Mad Forest

A Play from Romania

by Caryl Churchill

A SAMUEL FRENCH ACTING EDITION

SAMUEL FRENCH

FOUNDED 1830

New York Hollywood London Toronto

SAMUELFRENCH.COM

ISBN   978-0-573-69332-8   Printed   in   U.S.A.   #14957

MUSIC USE NOTE

Licensees are solely responsible for obtaining formal written permission from copyright owners to use copyrighted music in the performance of this play and are strongly cautioned to do so. If no such permission is obtained by the licensee, then the licensee must use only original music that the licensee owns and controls. Licensees are solely responsible and liable for all music clearances and shall indemnify the copyright owners of the play and their licensing agent, Samuel French, Inc., against any costs, expenses, losses and liabilities arising from the use of music by licensees.

IMPORTANT BILLING AND CREDIT REQUIREMENTS

All producers of *MAD FOREST* *must* give credit to the Author of the Play in all programs distributed in connection with performances of the Play, and in all instances in which the title of the Play appears for the purposes of advertising, publicizing or otherwise exploiting the Play and/or a production. The name of the Author *must* appear on a separate line on which no other name appears, immediately following the title and *must* appear in size of type not less than fifty percent of the size of the title type.

DIARY OF EVENTS

December 16–17
Demonstrations in Timosoara in support of Hungarian priest Laszlo Tokes.
Ceauseşcu visits Iran. Demonstrators in Timosoara shot.

December 21
Ceauseşcu's speech in Bucharest. He is shouted down. That night shooting.

December 22
Army goes over to people. Ceauseşcu escapes. TV station occupied. National Salvation Front formed. More shooting which continues for several days.

December 25
Ceauseşcu captured, tried by military tribunal and shot.

Mid-January
Director Mark Wing-Davey suggests Romania project with Central School students to writer Caryl Churchill.

Late January & February
Front announces it will stand in elections. Demonstrations against Front and Iliescu, and in support.

March 3–7
Director and writer go to Romania.

March 31–April 7
Director, writer, designer, lighting designer, 1 stage management and 10 acting students go to Romania, work with students at the Caragiale

Institute of Theatre and Cinema, and meet many other people.

May
Anti-Front demonstrators block centre of Bucharest.

May 20
Election. Iliescu and Front have large majorities.

May 21
Rehearsals begin

June 13
Miners enter Bucharest to crush anti-Front demonstrations. First performance of *Mad Forest* at Central School.

September 17
National Theatre, Bucharest. Discussions with audience.

MAD FOREST

On the plain where Bucharest now stands there
used to be "a large forest crossed by small muddy
streams ... It could only be crossed on foot and
was impenetrable for the foreigner who did not
know the paths ... The horsemen of the steppe
were compelled to go round it, and this difficulty,
which irked them so, is shown by the name ...
Teleorman—Mad Forest."

A Concise History of Romania,
Otetea and MacKenzie

PRODUCTION NOTE

Since the play goes from the difficulty of saying anything to everyone talking, don't be afraid of long silences. For instance, in Scene 1, the silence before Bogdan turns up the music was a good fifteen seconds in our production. Short scenes like 13 and 15 need to be given their weight. Don't add additional dialogue (for instance in queues, party or arrival in country) except in II, 6 where "etc." means there can be other things shouted by the spectators.

The queue scenes and execution scene should have as many people as are available. In the execution scene it is the violence of the spectators which is the main focus rather than the execution itself.

We didn't use a prop rat.

The Vampire was not dressed as a vampire.

In Part II (December) the language of the different characters varies with how well they speak English, and this should be reflected in their accents.

In the hospital and party scenes it is particularly important that the short scenes within them are not run together and that time has clearly passed.

Music. As in the text, the music after the opening poem becomes the music on the Vladu radio. It's not essential to do what we did with the music, but it may be helpful to know that at the end of the wedding scene we used a hymn to the Ceausescus and continued the music till everyone was in place for the beginning of December; at the end of December the whole company sang a verse from "Wake Up Romania" in Romanian, which then merged with a recording of it; we had music at the beginning of Part III. The party music in III, 8 should be western euro-pop. The dance music should be the lambada—this is not an arbitrary choice, it was the popular dance at the time. The nightmare scene and the very end of the play probably need sound.

Words for the poem at the beginning and words and music for "Wake Up Romania" can be got from Casarotto Ramsay Ltd., National House, 60-66 Wardour St., London, W1V 3HP, England.

Caryl Churchill and Mark Wing-Davey
March 1991

Mad Forest was first staged by students in their final year of training at the Central School of Speech and Drama, London, on 25 June 1990 with the cast as follows. It was subsequently performed at the National Theatre, Bucharest, from 17 September and opened at the Royal Court Theatre, London on 9 October 1990 with the same cast.

VLADU FAMILY

BOGDAN, an electrician	David MacCreedy
IRINA, a tramdriver	Lucy Cohu
their children:	
LUCIA, a primary school teacher	Nicola Gibson
FLORINA, a nurse	Victoria Alcock
GABRIEL, an engineer	David Mestecky
RODICA, Gabriel's wife	Sarah Ball
WAYNE, Lucia's bridegroom	Gordon Anderson
GRANDFATHER, Bogdan's father	Iain Hake
GRANDMOTHER, Bogdan's mother	Sara Ball
OLD AUNT, Bogdan's aunt	Iain Hake

ANTONESCU FAMILY

MIHAI, an architect	Gordon Anderson
FLAVIA, a teacher	Sarah Ball
RADU, an art student, their son	Mark Heal
GRANDMOTHER, Flavia's grandmother	Lucy Cohu
IANOŞ	Philip Glenister
SECURITATE MAN	Iain Hake
DOCTOR	Joseph Bennett
PRIEST	Iain Hake

(contd.)

ANGEL	Joseph Bennett
VAMPIRE	Iain Hake
DOG	Gordon Anderson
SOMEONE WITH SORE THROAT	Iain Hake
PATIENT	Joseph Bennett
TWO SOLDIERS	Ian Hake & Joseph Bennett
TOMA, age 8	David MacCreedy
GHOST	Joseph Bennett
WAITER	Joseph Bennett
PAINTER	Philip Glenister
GIRL STUDENT	Lucy Cohu
2 BOY STUDENTS	Joseph Bennett & David MacCreedy
TRANSLATOR	Gordon Anderson
BULLDOZER DRIVER	David Mestecky
SECURITATE OFFICER	Mark Heal
SOLDIER	Iain Hake
STUDENT DOCTOR	Nicola Gibson
FLOWER SELLER	Victoria Alcock
HOUSE PAINTER	Sarah Ball

PEOPLE IN QUEUES AND WEDDING GUESTS played by members of the company

Directed by Mark Wing-Davey
Designed by Antony McDonald
Lighting Design by Nigel H. Morgan

Mad Forest was presented in New York City by the New York Theatre Workshop, November 22 through December 29, 1991. It was directed by Mark Wing-Davey and had the following cast:

VLADU FAMILY

BOGDAN, an electrician	Lanny Flaherty
IRINA, a bus driver	Randy Danson
Their children:	
LUCIA, an elementary school teacher	Calista Flockhart
FLORINA, a nurse	Mary Mara
GABRIEL, an engineer	Tim Nelson

RODICA, Gabriel's wife	Mary Shultz
WAYNE, an American	Christopher McCann
GRANDFATHER, Bogdan's father	Joseph Siravo
GRANDMOTHER, Bogdan's mother	Mary Shultz
OLD AUNT, Bogdan's aunt	Joseph Siravo

ANTONESCU FAMILY

MIHAI, an architect	Christopher McCann
FLAVIA, a teacher	Mary Shultz
RADU, an art student, their son	Jake Weber
GRANDMOTHER, Flavia's grandmother	Randy Danson

IANOŞ	Garret Dillahunt
SECURITATE MAN, ANGEL, PATIENT,	
TOMA, GHOST, WAITER, DOCTOR,	
PRIEST, VAMPIRE, SOMEONE	
WITH SORE THROAT	Joseph Siravo
DOG	Christopher McCann

(contd.)

SOLDIERS in Rodica's nightmare	Lanny Flaherty, Joseph Siravo
PAINTER	Garret Dillahunt
GIRL STUDENT	Mary Mara
BOY STUDENTS	Rob Campbell, Tim Nelson
TRANSLATOR	Lanny Flaherty
BULLDOZER DRIVER	Christopher McCann
SECURITATE OFFICER	Joseph Siravo
SOLDIER	Jake Weber
STUDENT DOCTOR	Calista Flockhart
FLOWER SELLER	Randy Danson
HOUSE PAINTER	Mary Shultz

Other characters played by members of the company.

Set and Costume Designer: Marina Draghici
Lighting Designer: Christopher Akerlind
Sound Designer: Mark Bennett
Fight Director: David Leong
Dialect Coach: Deborah Hecht
Production Stage Manager: Thom Widmann
Production Manager: George Xenos
Casting: Wendy Ettinger
Dramaturg: Beth Schachter

PRONUNCIATION GUIDE

General notes: All R's are slightly trilled.
The U at the end of words is pronounced "oo."

ANTONIU	Ant-on-you
BARBU	Barr-boo
CONSTANTINESCU	Con-stan-tin-esk-oo
BOGDAN	Bog-dan
CALLEA	Cal (as in pal)-ay-a
CEAUSEȘCU	Chow-oo-shes-koo
CHIRITA	Ki (as in kill)-ree-tza
CLAUDIU	Clo (as in now)-oo-dee-you
CONSTANTINESCU	Con-stan-tin-esk-oo
CORNEL	Corn-ell
CORNELIA	Corn-ay-lya
CRAIOVA	Cry-oh-va
DEDILIUC	Dead-eel-yook (as in book)
DRAGAN	Drag-ann
FLAVIA	Flah-vee-a
FLORINA	Flo (as in on) reen-a
GABRIEL	Gab (as in cab) ree-el
GHEORGHE	Gay-or-gay
IANOȘ	Yan (as in can)-osh (as in gosh)
ILEANA	Ill-ay-ah-na
ILIE	Ill-yah (as in pay)
IRINA	I (as in inn) ree-na
JOS	J as in French "je," Joss (oss as in moss)
LUCIA	Loo-chya
MARGARETA	Mar-ga (as in gap)-rett-a
MARIN	Ma (as in man)-rin (as in bin)
MIHAI	Mee-high

MORARU	Mo (as in on) rah-roo
RADU	Rad (as in mad)-oo
RODICA	Rod (as in cod) ee-ka
RUSU	Roo-soo
SECURITATE	Seck-oo-ree-tah-tay
STEFAN	Shtef (as in step)-ann
TIMIȘOARA	Tim-i-shwara
TOMA	Tome (as in home) -a
VITTORIA	Vitt-or-ee-a

NOTES ON LAYOUT

A speech usually follows the one immediately before it. BUT:

(1) When one character starts speaking before the other has finished the point of interruption is marked / and the first character continues talking regardless:

e.g.
GABRIEL. They came to the office yesterday and gave us one of their usual pep talks and at the end one of them took me aside / and said we'd
IRINA. Wait
GABRIEL. like to see you tomorrow. So I know what that meant ...

(2) Sometimes two speakers interrupt at once while the first speaker continues:*

e.g.
FLAVIA. Why don't the Front tell the truth and admit they're communists? / *Nothing to be
MIHAI. Because they're not.
RADU. *I don't care what they're called, it's the same people.
FLAVIA. ashamed of in communism ...
Here both MIHAI and RADU interrupt FLAVIA at the same point.

I. LUCIA'S WEDDING

The company recite, smiling, a poem in Romanian in
*   praise of Elena Ceauşescu.*
Stirring ROMANIAN MUSIC.
Each scene is announced by one of the company reading
*   from a phrasebook as if an English tourist, first in*
*   Romanian, then in English, and again in Romanian.*

1. Lucia are patru ouǎ. Lucia has four eggs.

MUSIC continues. BOGDAN and IRINA VLADU sit in
*   silence.*
BOGDAN turns up the music on the radio very loud. He
*   sits looking at IRINA.*
IRINA puts her head close to BOGDAN's and talks quickly
*   and quietly, to convince him.*
He argues back, she insists, he gets angry. We can't hear
*   anything they say.*
They stop talking and sit with the music blaring.
*   BOGDAN is about to speak when FLORINA and*
*   LUCIA come in, laughing.*
They stop laughing and look at BOGDAN and IRINA.
IRINA turns the radio down low.
LUCIA produces four eggs with a flourish. IRINA kisses
*   her.*
BOGDAN ignores her.
LUCIA produces a packet of American cigarettes.
FLORINA laughs.

LUCIA opens the cigarettes and offers them to IRINA. She hesitates, then puts out her cigarette and takes one. FLORINA takes one.
BOGDAN ignores them.
LUCIA offers a cigarette to BOGDAN, he shakes his head.
LUCIA takes a cigarette. They sit smoking.
BOGDAN finishes his cigarette. He sits without smoking. Then he takes a cigarette.
LUCIA and FLORINA laugh.
BOGDAN picks up an egg and breaks it on the floor.
IRINA gathers the other eggs to safety.
LUCIA and FLORINA keep still.
IRINA turns the radio up loud and is about to say something.
BOGDAN turns the radio completely off. IRINA ignores him and smokes.
FLORINA gets a cup and spoon and scrapes up what she can of the egg off the floor.
LUCIA keeps still.

2. Cine are un chibrit? Who has a match?

ANTONESCU family, noticeably better off than the VLADUS.
MIHAI thinking and making notes, FLAVIA correcting exercise books, RADU drawing.
They sit in silence for some time. When they talk they don't look up from what they're doing.

MIHAI. He came today.

FLAVIA. That's exciting.

RADU. Did he make you change it?

MIHAI. He had a very interesting recommendation. The arch should be this much higher.

RADU. And the columns?

MIHAI. We will make an improvement to the spacing of the columns.

FLAVIA. That sounds good.

(They go on working.
The LIGHTS go out. They are resigned, almost indifferent.
RADU takes a match and lights a candle.
They sit in CANDLELIGHT in silence.)

RADU. I don't see why.

FLAVIA. We've said no.

RADU. If I put if off for a year or two till after the wedding. I / could —

FLAVIA. No.

RADU. It's not her fault if her sister —

MIHAI. The whole family. No. Out of the question. *(Pause.)* There are plenty of other girls, Radu.

(They sit in silence.
The LIGHTS come on.
FLAVIA blows out the candle and snuffs it with her
*   fingers.*
They all start reading again.)

RADU. So is that the third time he's made you change it?

(MIHAI doesn't reply. They go on working.)

3. Ea are o scrisoare din Statele Unite. She has a letter from the United States.

again w/ America + Lucia

LUCIA is reading an airmail letter, smiling. She kisses the letter. She puts it away. FLORINA comes in from work.

    LUCIA. Tired?

(Pause. FLORINA is taking off her shoes.)

    LUCIA. I'm sorry.

(FLORINA smiles and shrugs.)

    LUCIA. No but all of you ... because of me and Wayne.
    FLAVIA. You love him.

(LUCIA takes out the letter and offers it to FLORINA. FLORINA hesitates. LUCIA insists. FLORINA reads the letter, she is serious. LUCIA watches her. FLORINA gives the letter back.)

    LUCIA. And Radu? Have you seen him lately?

(FLORINA shrugs.)

4. Elevii ascultă lecţia. The pupils listen to the lesson.

FLAVIA speaks loudly and confidently to her pupils.

FLAVIA. Today we are going to learn about a life dedicated to the happiness of the people and noble ideas of socialism.

The new history of the motherland is like a great river with its fundamental starting point in the biography of our general secretary, the president of the republic, Comrade Nicolae Ceausescu, and it flows through the open spaces of the important dates and problems of contemporary humanity. Because it's evident to everybody that linked to the personality of this great son of the nation is everything in the country that is most durable and harmonious, the huge transformations taking place in all areas of activity, the ever more vigorous and ascendant path towards the highest stages of progress and civilisation. He is the founder of the country. More, he is the founder of man. For everything is being built for the sublime development of man and country, for their material and spiritual well-being.

He started his revolutionary activity in the earliest years of his adolescence in conditions of danger and illegality, therefore his life and struggle cannot be detached from the most burning moments of the people's fight against fascism and war to achieve the ideals of freedom and aspirations of justice and progress.

We will learn the biography under four headings.
1. village of his birth and prison
2. revolution
3. leadership
4. the great personality of Comrade Nicolae Ceauşescu.

5. Cumpărăm carne. We are buying meat.

*RADU is in a queue of people with shopping bags. They
     stand a long time in silence.
Someone leaves a bag with a bottle in it to mark the place
     goes.
They go on standing.*

     RADU. (*Whispers loudly.*) Down with Ceauşescu.

*(The woman in front of him starts to look round, then
     pretends she hasn't heard. The man behind pretends he
     hasn't heard and casually steps slightly away from
     RADU.
Two people towards the head of the queue look round and
     RADU looks round as if wondering who spoke.
They go on queueing.)*

**6. Doi oameni stau la soare. Two men are
sitting in the sun.**

BOGDAN and SECURITATE MAN.

SECURITATE. Do you love your country?

(BOGDAN nods.)

SECURITATE. And how do you show it? *(Pause.)* You love your country, how do you show it?

(BOGDAN is about to speak. He stops. He is about to speak.)

SECURITATE. You encourage your daughter to marry an American.
BOGDAN. No.

(Pause.)

SECURITATE. It can take two years to get a passport. *(Silence.)* Your daughter was trained as an elementary school teacher, she can no longer be employed. Romania has wasted resources that could have benefited a young woman with a sense of duty. *(Silence.)* I understand your wife works as a bus driver and has recently been transferred to a depot in the south of the city which doubles the time she has to travel to work. You are an electrician, you have been a foreman for some time but alas no longer. Your son is an engineer and is so far doing well. Your other daughter is a nurse. So far there is nothing against her except her sister. *(Pause.)* I'm sure you are eager to show that your family are patriots. *(Silence. BOGDAN looks away.)* When they know your daughter wants to marry an American, people may confide their own shameful secrets. They may mistakenly think you are someone who has sympathy with foreign regimes. Your other children may make undesirable friends who think you're prepared to listen to what they say. They will be right. You will listen. (*Pause. BOGDAN is about to say something but doesn't.*) What? (*Pause.*) Your colleagues will know you have been demoted and will wrongly suppose that you are short of money. As a patriot you may not have noticed how anyone out of favour attracts the friendship of irresponsible bitter people who feel slighted. Be friendly. (*Pause.*) What a beautiful day. What a beautiful country. (*Silence. BOGDAN looks at him.*) You will make a report once a week.

7. Ascultaţi? Are you listening?

LUCIA and a DOCTOR.
While they talk the DOCTOR writes on a piece of paper, pushes it over to LUCIA, who writes a reply, and he writes again.

DOCTOR. You're a slut. You've brought this on yourself. The only thing to be said in its favour is that one more child is one more worker.

LUCIA. Yes, I realise that.

DOCTOR. There is no abortion in Romania. I am shocked that you even think of it. I am appalled that you dare suggest I might commit this crime.

LUCIA. Yes, I'm sorry. (*LUCIA gives the doctor an envelope thick with money and some more money.*)

DOCTOR. Can you get married?

LUCIA. Yes.
DOCTOR. Good. Get married.

(The DOCTOR writes again, LUCIA nods.)

DOCTOR. I can do nothing for you. Goodbye.
LUCIA. *(Smiles. She makes her face serious again.)*
Goodbye.

8. Sticla cu vin este pe masă. The bottle of wine is on the table.

RADU, GABRIEL and IANOS with a bottle of wine. They are in public so they keep their voices down.

IANOS. He died and went to heaven and St. Peter says, "God wants a word with you." So he goes in to see God and God says, "I hear you think you're greater than me." And he says, "Yes, I am." And God says, "Right, who made the sun?" "You did." "Who made the stars?" "You did." "Who made the earth?" "You did." "Who made all the people and all the animals and all the trees and all the / plants and —
RADU. "And all the wine."
IANOS. "And everything?" And he said, "You did, God." And God says, "Then how can you possible be greater than me?" And he says, "All these things, what did you make them from?" And God said, "Chaos, I made it all out of chaos." "There you are," he said, "I made chaos."

RADU. Hey, Ianos, Ianos. A cosmonaut leaves a message for his wife. "Gone to Mars, back in two weeks." Two weeks later he comes back and his wife has left him a message. "Gone shopping, don't know when I'll be back."

GABRIEL. A man wants a car and he saves up his money and at last he's able to buy a Trabant. He's very proud of it. And he's driving along in his little Trabant and he stops at the traffic lights and bang, a car crashes into the back of it. So he leaps out very angry, and it's a black car with a short license plate, but he's so angry he doesn't care and he starts banging on the hood. Then a big dump truck stops behind the black car and the driver gets out and he takes a crowbar and he starts smashing the back of the black car. And the Securitate man gets out of his battered black car and he says to the truck driver, "What's going on? I can understand him being upset because I hit his car, but what's the matter with you?" And the driver says, "Sorry, I thought it had started."

9. **Cerul este albastru. The sky is blue.**

An ANGEL and a PRIEST

ANGEL. Don't be ashamed. When people come into church they are free. Even if they know there are Securitate in church with them. Even if some churches are demolished, so long as there are some churches standing. Even if you say hey, Ceausescu, hey, Ceausescu, because the Romanian church is a church of freedom. Not outer freedom of course but inner freedom.

(Silence. The PRIEST sits gazing at the Angel.)

PRIEST. This is so sweet, like looking at the colour blue, like looking at the sky when you're a child lying on your back, you stare out at the blue but you're going in, further and further in away from the world, that's what it's like knowing I can talk to you. Someone says something, you say something back, you're called to a police station, that happened to my brother. So it's not safe to go out to people and when you can't go out sometimes you find you can't go in, I'm afraid to go inside myself, perhaps there's nothing there, I just keep still. But I can talk to you, no one's ever known an angel work for the Securitate, I go out into the blue and I sink down and down inside myself, and yes then I am free inside, I can fly about in that blue, that is what the church can give people, they can fly about inside in that blue.

ANGEL. So when the Romanian church writes a letter to the other Christian churches apologising for not taking a stand / against —

PRIEST. Don't talk about it. I'd just managed to forget.

ANGEL. Don't be ashamed. There was no need for them to write the letter because there's no question of taking a stand, it's not the job of the church / to —

PRIEST. Everyone will think we're cowards.

ANGEL. No no no. Flying about in the blue.

PRIEST. Yes. Yes. (*Pause.*) You've never been political?

ANGEL. Very little. The Iron Guard used to be rather charming and called themselves the League of the

Archangel Michael and carried my picture about. They had
lovely processions. So I dabbled.

PRIEST. But they were fascists.

ANGEL. They were mystical.

PRIEST. The Iron Guard threw Jews out of windows in
'37, my father remembers it. He shouted and they beat him
up.

ANGEL. Politics, you see. Their politics weren't very
pleasant. I try to keep clear of the political side. You
should do the same.

(Pause.)

PRIEST. I don't trust you any more.

ANGEL. That's a pity. Who else can you trust?
(Pause.) Would you rather feel ashamed? *(Pause.)* Or are
you going to take some kind of action, surely not?

(Silence.)

PRIEST. Comfort me.

**10. Acesta este fratele nostru. This is our
brother.**

*BOGDAN, IRINA, LUCIA, FLORINA, sitting in the dark
with candles. IRINA is sewing LUCIA's wedding dress.
GABRIEL arrives, excited.*

GABRIEL. Something happened today. / They came to

IRINA. Wait. (*Moves to turn on the radio, then remembers it isn't working.*)

GABRIEL. the office yesterday and gave us their usual pep talk and at the end one of them took me aside / and said

IRINA. Wait.

GABRIEL. we'd like to see you tomorrow. So I knew what that meant, they were going to ask me / to do

IRINA. Wait, stop, there's no power.

GABRIEL. something for them. I prayed all night I'd be strong enough to say no, I was so afraid I'd be persuaded, / I've never been brave. So I went in and they said …

IRINA. Gaby, stop, be quiet.

FLORINA. No, what if they do hear it, they know what they did.

GABRIEL. And they said, "What is patriotism?" I said, "It's doing all you can, working as hard as possible." And they said, / "We thought you might not understand

BOGDAN. Gabriel.

FLORINA. No, let him.

(*IRINA puts her hands over her ears. But after a while she starts to listen again.*)

GABRIEL. patriotism because your sister and this and this, but if you're a patriot you'll want to help us. And I said, "Of course I'd like to help you." and then I actually remembered listen to this, 'As Comrade Ceausescu says, "For each and every citizen work is an honorary fundamental duty. Each of us should demonstrate high professional probity, competence, creativity, devotion and passion in our work." And because I'm a patriot I work so hard that I can't think about anything else, I wouldn't be able to listen to what my colleagues talk about because I have to concentrate. I work right through the lunch hour." And I stuck to it and they couldn't do anything. And I'm so happy because I've put myself on the other side, I hardly knew there was one. They made me promise never to tell anyone they'd asked me, and they made me sign something, I didn't care by then, I'd won, so I signed it, not my wife or my parents, it said that specifically because they know what the first thing is you'd do, and of course I'm doing it because I don't care, I'm going straight home to Rodica to tell her, I'm so happy, and I've come to share it with you because I knew you'd be proud of me.

IRINA. But you signed. You shouldn't tell us. I didn't hear.

FLORINA. (*Kisses Gabriel.*) But Radu's right to keep away from us.

(*Pause.*)

BOGDAN. You're a good boy.

GABRIEL. I was shaking. The first thing when I went in they said —

(*BOGDAN holds up his hand and GABRIEL stops. Pause.*)

LUCIA. What if I don't get my passport?

11. Uite! Look!

Not prop rat

A SOLDIER and a WAITER stand smoking in the street.
Suddenly one of them shouts "Rat!" and they chase it.
RADU, IANOS and GABRIEL pass and join in. The rat
is kicked about like a football. Then RADU, IANOS
and GABRIEL go on their way and the SOLDIER and
the WAITER go back to smoking.

12. Eu o vizitez pe nepoata mea. I am visiting my granddaughter.

FLAVIA and MIHAI sitting silently over their work.
FLAVIA'S GRANDMOTHER, who is dead. She is an
elegant woman in her 50s.

GRANDMOTHER. Flavia, your life will soon be over.
You're nearly as old as I was when you were a little girl.
You thought I was old then but you don't think you're old.

FLAVIA. Yes I do. I look at my son's friends and I
know I'm old.

GRANDMOTHER. No, you still think your life hasn't
started. You think it's ahead.

FLAVIA. Everyone feels like that.

GRANDMOTHER. How do you know? Who do you
talk to? Your closest friend is your grandmother and I'm
dead, Flavia, don't forget that or you really will be mad.

FLAVIA. You want me to live in the past? I do, I
remember being six years old in the mountains, isn't that
what old people do?

GRANDMOTHER. You remember being a child, Flavia, because you're childish. You remember expecting a treat.

FLAVIA. Isn't that good? Imagine still having hope at my age. I admire myself.

GRANDMOTHER. You're pretending this isn't your life. You think it's going to happen some other time. When you're dead you'll realise you were alive now. When I was your age the war was starting. I welcomed the Nazis because I thought they'd protect us from the Russians and I welcomed the Communists because I thought they'd protect us from the Germans. I had no principles. My husband was killed. But at least I knew that was what happened to me. There were things I did. I did them. Or sometimes I did nothing. It was me doing nothing.

(Silence.)

FLAVIA. Mihai.

MIHAI. Mm?

FLAVIA. Do you ever think ... if you think of something you'll do ... do you ever think you'll be young when you do it? Do you think I'll do that next time I'm twenty? Not really exactly think it because of course it doesn't make sense but almost ... not exactly think it but ...

(MIHAI shakes his head and goes back to his work.)

FLAVIA. Yes, my life is over.

GRANDMOTHER. I didn't say that.

FLAVIA. I don't envy the young, there's nothing ahead
for them either. I'm nearer dying and that's fine.

GRANDMOTHER. You're not used to listening. What
did I say?

(Pause.)

FLAVIA. But nobody's living. You can't blame me.
GRANDMOTHER. You'd better start.
FLAVIA. No, Granny, it would hurt.
GRANDMOTHER. Well.

(Silence.)

FLAVIA. Mihai.

(MIHAI goes on working.)

FLAVIA. Mihai.

(He looks up.
Silence.)

13. Ce oră este? What's the time?

LUCIA and IANOS standing in silence with their arms
round each other.
She looks at her watch, he puts his hand over it.
They go on standing.

14. Unde este troleibuzul? Where is the trolley?

People waiting for a bus, including RADU.
FLORINA joins the queue. She doesn't see him.
He sees her. He looks away.
She sees him without him noticing, she looks away.
He looks at her again, they see each other and greet each
    other awkwardly They look away.
RADU goes up to her.

    RADU. How are you?
    FLORINA. Fine.
    RADU. And your family?
    FLORINA. Fine, and yours?
    RADU. So when's Lucia's wedding?
    FLORINA. You know when it is.

(They stand apart waiting for the bus.)

15. Pe Irina o doare capul. Irina has a headache.

LUCIA is trying on her wedding dress, helped by IRINA.

16. Lucia are o coroană de aur. Lucia has a golden crown.

The wedding. LUCIA and WAYNE are being married by
the PRIEST, BOGDAN, IRINA, FLORINA,
GABRIEL and RODICA. Other guests.
Two wedding crowns. The PRIEST crosses WAYNE with
a crown, saying:

PRIEST. The servant of God Wayne is crowned for the
handmaid of God Lucia, in the name of the father, and of
the son, and of the holy spirit.
    ALL. (*Sing.*) Amen.

(This is repeated three times, then the PRIEST puts the
crown on LUCIA's head.
MUSIC.)

II DECEMBER

None of the characters in this section are the characters in the play that began in part I. They are all Romanians speaking to us in English with Romanian accents. Each behaves as if the others are not there and each is the only one telling what happened.

PAINTER. My name is Valentin Bărbat, I am a painter. I hope to go to the Art Institute. I like to paint horses. Other things too but I like horses. On December 20 my girlfriend got a call, go to the Palace Square. People were wearing black armbands for Timisoara. There was plenty of people but no courage. Nothing happened that day and we went home.

GIRL STUDENT. My name's Natalia Moraru, I'm a student. On the 21st of December I had a fight with my mother at breakfast about something trivial and I went out in a rage. There was nothing unusual, some old men talking, a few plainclothes policemen, they think they're clever but everyone knows who they are because of their squashed faces.

TRANSLATOR. I'm Dimitru Constantinescu, I work as a translator in a translation agency. On the 21st we were listening to the radio in the office to hear Ceausescu's speech. It was frightfully predictable. People had been brought from factories and institutes on buses and he wanted their approval for putting down what he called the hooligans in Timisoara. Then suddenly we heard boos and the radio went dead. So we knew something had happened. We were awfully startled. Everyone was shaking.

BOY STUDENT 1. My name is Cornel Drăgan, I am a student and I watch the speech on TV. The TV went dead, I was sure at last something happens so I go out to see.

GIRL STUDENT. I went into a shop and heard something had been organised by Ceaușescu and the roads were blocked by traffic. I thought I'd walk to the People's Palace.

BULLDOZER DRIVER. My name is Ilie Barbu. I can work many machines. I work in all the country to build hospitals and schools. Always build, never pull down. In December I work at the People's Palace, I drive a bulldozer. There are always many Securitate and today they make us scared because they are scared.

BOY STUDENT 1. I see people running away and I try to stop them to ask what is happening but nobody has courage to talk. At last someone says, Let's hope it has started.

BOY STUDENT 2. Well, I'm Stefan Rusu, in fact I come from Craiova, I only live in Bucharest since September to study. On the 21 no one in our zone knew what was going on. My uncle had just come back from Iran so my sister and I went to meet him and my mother. In the Callea Vittoria I saw Securitate who were upset, they were whispering. Well in fact Securitate have come to me when I was working and asked me to write reports on my colleagues. I agreed because I would get a passport and go to America, but I never wrote anything bad to get someone in trouble. Nobody knew I did this with Securitate. Now I could see the Securitate in the street were scared. Cars were breaking the rules and driving the wrong way up the road. We went to the Hotel Dorobanti but we were not allowed to have a meal. We were whispering, my mother told us she had been in the square and heard people booing.

STUDENT 1. I got to the square and people are shouting against Ceauşescu, shouting "Today in Timisoara, tomorrow in all the country." I look at their lips to believe they say it. I see a friend and at first I don't know him, his face has changed, and when he looks at me I know my face is changed also.

DOCTOR. My name is Ileana Chiriţa. I'm a student doctor. I come to this hospital from school, we must get six months' practical. The 21 was a normal day on duty, I didn't know anything.

GIRL STUDENT. On my way to the People's Palace I saw people waiting in line for a new murder mystery that had just been published, so as I was feeling guilty about my mother I decided to try and buy one, murder mysteries are her favourite books. So I waited in line to get the book, and at about one o'clock I went home.

BULLDOZER DRIVER. I leave work to get my son from school and I don't go back to work, I go to the Palace Square.

STUDENT 1. There were two camps, army and people, but nobody shooting. Some workers from the People's Palace come with construction material to make barricades. More and more people come, we are pushed together.

DOCTOR. On my way home in the afternoon there was a woman crying because she lost her handbag, the other women comfort her saying, "It could be worse, people were crushed and lost their shoes, don't cry for such a small thing."

SECURITATE. Claudiu Brad, I am an officer in Securitate. In everything I did I think I was right, including the 21. I went to military high school because I like uniforms. My family has no money for me to study but I did well. I went to the Officers School of Securitate and got in the external department, which is best, the worst ones go in the fire service. Nobody knows I am in Securitate except one friend I have since I am three years old. I have no other friends but I like women and recruit them sometimes with clothes. On December 21 I am taking the pulse of the street in plain clothes with a walkie-talkie hidden. My district is Rossetti Place. I report every three hours if the crowd move their position, how could they be made calm, what they want.

SOLDIER. My name is Gheorghe Marin. I am in army from September. My mother is in house, my father mechanic in railway. December I am near airport. They say Hungarians come from Hungary into Romania, we must shoot them. They give us four magazines. Before, we work in the fields, we have one lessons to shoot. 21 we are in trenches, we have spades to dig. We wait something, we don't know what. We don't know what happen in Bucharest.

GIRL STUDENT. I'd planned to go see a movie with a friend but in the afternoon my father said I must ring up and pretend to be ill, then my friend rang and said that she is ill. I wanted to go out and my father said I couldn't go alone. I thought of an excuse — we had to have some bread, so we went out together. There were a lot of people moving from Union Place towards University Place and I heard someone shout, "Down with the Dictator." I was very confused. This was opposed to the policy of the leading forces. A man came up and asked what was happening but my father pulled me away because he realised the man was a provoker who starts arguments and then reports the people who get involved. My father insisted we go home, I said he was a coward and began to cry. He said if he was single he would behave differently.

BULLDOZER DRIVER. In the square there is much army and tanks. My son is six years old, I am scared for him. I take him home and we watch what happens on TV with my wife and daughter.

STUDENT 2. About five o'clock we heard people shouting "Jos Ceauşescu." My uncle wanted to go home to Cluj. Walking back I noticed it was 99% young people in the square with police and soldiers near them and I thought "That's the end for them." At home we tried to avoid the topic and get it out of our minds.

STUDENT 1. There are vans bringing drink and I tell people not to drink because Securitate wants to get us drunk so we look bad. In the evening we tried to make a barricade in Rosetti Place. We set fire to a truck.

SECURITATE. There are barricades and cars burning in my district, I report it. Later the army shoot the people and drive tank in them. I go off duty.

HOUSE PAINTER. My name is Margareta Antoniu, my work is house painter. I paint the windows on the big apartment buildings. I come back to work just now because I have a baby. The 21, the evening, I come home from a village with my children and my husband says it is happening. We expect it because of Timisoara. He hear tanks and shooting like an earthquake. We are happy someone fight for our people.

DOCTOR. My husband was away to visit his parents and I felt lonely. My mother phoned and warned me to stay home and said, "Listen to the cassette"—this is our code for Radio Free Europe.

FLOWER SELLER. My name is Cornelia Dediliuc. I am a flower seller, 22 years. Three children, 7, 4 and 2. I have a great pain because my mother die three weeks. My husband is very good, we meet when I am 14, before him I know only school and home. Before I tell you December I tell you something before in my family. My son who is 4 is 2, we live in a small room, I cook, I go out and my child pull off the hot water and hurt very bad. I come in and see, I have my big child 5 my hands on his neck because he not take care. Now I have illness, I have headache, and sometimes I don't know what I do. When the revolution start I am home with my children. The shooting is very big. I hold my children and stay there.

PAINTER. When we heard shooting we went out, and we stayed near the Intercontinental Hotel till nearly midnight. I had an empty soul. I didn't know who I was.

STUDENT 1. They shot tracer bullets with the real bullets to show they were shooting high. At first people don't believe they will shoot in the crowd again after Timisoara.

PAINTER. I saw a tank drive into the crowd, a man's head was crushed. When people were killed like that more people came in front of the tanks.

FLOWER SELLER. My husband come home scared, he has seen dead people. I say him please not to go out again because the children.

GIRL STUDENT. At about 11 my family began to argue so I went to my room. I heard shooting and called my father. He wouldn't let me open the shutter but through a crack I saw a wounded army officer running across the street screaming.

PAINTER. It's enough to see one person dead to get empty of feeling.

FLOWER SELLER. But I sleep and he goes out. I can't see something because the window of the apartment is not that way but I hear the shooting.

STUDENT 2. My mother, sister and I all slept in the same room that night because we were scared.

DOCTOR. The block was very quiet. Lights were on very late. I could hear other people listening to the radio.

GIRL STUDENT. I sat up till four in the morning. I wanted to go out but my father had locked the door and hidden the key.

STUDENT 1. At four in the morning I telephone my mother and tell her peoples are being killed.

PAINTER. That night it seems it must be all over. I hope it will go on tomorrow but don't know how.

SECURITATE. In the night the army cleaned the blood off the streets and painted the walls and put tar on the ground where there were stains from the blood so everything was clean.

STUDENT 1. At six in the morning there is new tar on the road but I see blood and something that is a piece of skin. Someone puts down a white cloth on the blood and peoples throw money, flowers, candles, that is the beginning of the shrines.

DOCTOR. On my way to work on the morning of the 22 there were broken windows and people washing the street.

BULLDOZER DRIVER. On the 22 I go back to work. I am afraid I am in trouble with Securitate because I leave work the day before but nobody says nothing.

DOCTOR. At the hospital no one knew what had happened but there were 14 dead and 19 wounded. There were two kinds of wounds, normal bullet wounds and bullets that explode when they strike something and break bones in little pieces, there is no way of repairing them.

HOUSE PAINTER. About 7 o'clock I take a shower. I hear a noise in the street. I look out, I see thousands of workers from the Industrial Platforms. I am wet, I have no clothes, I stay to watch. They are more and more, two three kilometres. Now I know Ceausescu is finish.

DOCTOR. At about 8 I saw out of the window people going towards University Square holding flags. They pass a church and suddenly they all knelt down in silence. My colleagues began to say, He will fall. An old doctor, 64 years old, climbed to a dangerous place to get down Ceausescu's picture and we all cheered. We heard on the radio the General in charge of the Army had killed himself and been announced a traitor. We kept treating patients and running back to the radio.

STUDENT 2. We heard that the General committed suicide and there was a state of emergency declared. I thought everything is lost.

GIRL STUDENT. I insisted we go out. My father dressed like a bride taking a long time.

FLOWER SELLER. I go to the market to get food and many people are going to the centre. I watch them go by. I am sorry I get married so young.

TRANSLATOR. I went to work as usual but there was only one colleague in my office. We heard shots so we went out. I've noticed in films people scatter away from gunfire but here people came out saying, "What's that?" People were shouting, "Come with us," so we went in the courtyard and shouted too.

GIRL STUDENT. We hadn't gone far when we saw a crowd of people with banners with Jos Ceausescu, shouting, "Come and join us." They were low class men so we didn't know if we could trust them. I suggested we cross the street so no one could say we were with them.

TRANSLATOR. I heard people shouting, "Down with · Ceauşescu," for the first time. It was a wonderful feeling to say those words, Jos Ceauşescu.

GIRL STUDENT. Suddenly there was a huge crowd with young people. For the first time I saw the flag with the hole cut out of it. I began to cry, I felt ashamed I hadn't done anything. My father agreed to go on but not with the crowd.

STUDENT 2. Then I saw students singing with flags with holes in them and I thought, Surely this is the end. I walked on the sidewalk beside them, quickly looking to the side for an escape route like a wild animal.

TRANSLATOR. I had promised my wife to take care. We were walking towards the tanks and I was quailing in my boots. But when you're with other people you keep walking on.

GIRL STUDENT. We came to University Place. For the first time I saw blood, it was smeared on a wooden cross. It's one thing to hear shooting but another to see blood. There were police in front of the Intercontinental Hotel. But in a crowd you disappear and feel stronger.

TRANSLATOR. Then I saw there were flowers in the guns.

GIRL STUDENT. I saw a tank with a soldier holding a red carnation.

TRANSLATOR. Everyone was hugging and kissing each other, you were kissing a chap you'd never seen before.

GIRL STUDENT. And when I looked again the police had vanished.

STUDENT 2. I saw people climbing on army vehicles, I thought they'd taken them from the soldiers, then I realised the soldiers were driving and I heard people shouting, "The army is with us." Then I started to cry and I shouted too, "The army is with us."

TRANSLATOR. There are no words in Romanian or English for how happy I was.

SECURITATE. On the 22 the army went over to the side of the people. I gave my pistol to an army officer and both magazines were full. That's why I'm here now. I had no more superiors and I wanted to get home. I caught the train and stayed in watching what happened on TV.

HOUSE PAINTER. We leave our six children with my mother and we follow some tanks with people on them. They are go to the TV station. We are there with the first people who make revolution.

BULLDOZER DRIVER. I work till half past ten or eleven, then I see tanks not with army, with men on them. I think I will take the bulldozer. But when I get to the gates my boss says, "There is no need, Ceausescu is no more, Ceausescu nu mai e." I see no Securitate so I go home to my family.

DOCTOR. Out of the window I saw a silver helicopter and pieces of paper falling—we thought the people had won and they were celebration papers.

GIRL STUDENT. There were leaflets thrown down from helicopters say, Go home and spend Christmas with your family.

DOCTOR. A boo went up outside when people saw what they said.

GIRL STUDENT. Suddenly I heard bangbang and I thought my heart would explode, but it was small children throwing celebration crackers against the walls. My father had an attack of cramps and couldn't move any further.

STUDENT 1. In the Palace Square when the tanks turn round we are afraid they will fire on us again. But they turn towards Ceausescu's balcony.

STUDENT 2. I saw books and papers thrown down from the balcony and I thought I must do something so I went to the radio station. I heard people singing "Wake Up Romanian," and realised it was a victory.

DOCTOR. About 12:30 I heard on the radio, "Wake Up Romania," the anthem which used to be banned, and announcers who apologise for not telling the truth, they had been made to lie. Everyone began to cry and laugh. The doctors and the orderlies were equal.

GIRL STUDENT. We saw an appeal on TV at a friend's house for blood so I went to the hospital with our friend's son-in-law. There were hundreds of people waiting to give blood but only fifty bottles, luckily I was able to give blood.

STUDENT 2. I bought some champagne and went home to my family to celebrate.

DOCTOR. I went home about 3 and my husband has bought 6 bottles of champagne and we called our neighbours in. For the first time in my life I felt free to laugh.

GIRL STUDENT. We went to the TV station, it was surrounded by cars beeping, soldiers wearing armbands to show they were with the people. We were told the water was poisoned by Securitate so I ran to buy some milk so my doggie could have something to drink.

STUDENT 1. In the afternoon I go to meet my mother when she comes out of school. Everyone is shouting Ole ole ole ole and the cars they honk their horns. Then I go to see my grandmother to show her I am all right.

(Pause.)

PAINTER. That night the terror shooting started. There was no quiet place.

TRANSLATOR. When the terror shooting started, I was at home and heard it. My legs buckled, I vomited, I couldn't go out. It took me weeks to get over that.

STUDENT 1. About 7 o'clock we heard on the radio, "Help, our building is being attacked." So I went out again.

HOUSE PAINTER. At the radio station I am scared, my husband says, "Why you come then?" Terroristi shoot from a building and my husband goes with men inside and catch them. There are many wounded and I help. I am the only woman.

SOLDIER. They say us it is not Hungarians. It is terroristi. We guard the airport. We shoots anything, we shoots our friend. I want to stay alive.

PAINTER. They are asking on TV for people to defend the TV station. My girlfriend and I go out. We stop a truck of young people and ask where they're going, they say,

"We are going to die." They say it like that. We can do nothing there, everyone knows it.

STUDENT 1. There was a gypsy who had a gun and he says "Come with me, I want people strong with courage." He says we must go to the factory of August 23 where they have guns for the guards. The Romanian people are cowards and have no courage to get in the truck, but at last we go to the factory. There are more than one hundred peoples but only 28 get guns, I get one, they say "Be careful and come back with the gun." Then we go to a police station because we know they are on the sides of the people and we ask for bullets. At first they don't want to give them, they say, "We need them to defend our building." We say, "Give us at least one bullet each to be of some use."

STUDENT 2. People were shouting, "Come with us," but I thought, "It's a romantic action, it's useless to go and fight and die." I thought I was a coward to be scared. But I thought, "I will die like a fool protecting someone I don't know. How can I stop bullets with my bare hands? It's the job of the army, I can do nothing, I will just die." So I went home.

STUDENT 1. At the TV station I am behind the wall of a house and they shoot across me from both sides. I go into a house, the terroristi they are gone, I telephone my mother to tell her where I am. If I stay ten minutes longer I am dead because they shoot that house. In the street a boy stands up and is shot. A month later is his eighteenth birthday. I ask myself if he is shot by our soldiers. I am standing looking around, bullets are flying. After a while you don't feel scared.

PAINTER. My girlfriend and I were at the TV station. I didn't know who we were fighting with or how bad it was. I was just acting to save our lives. It is terrible to hate and not to be able to do something real.

GIRL STUDENT. That evening I wanted to put on my army clothes and go out and shoot—I got three out of three in the shooting test when I was in the army. But my father had locked the door again and hidden the key.

HOUSE PAINTER. At ten o'clock we go back to the TV station with some bread.

STUDENT 1. A lot of people bring tea and food though they didn't know if there will be better days and more to eat. They bring things they save for Christmas. Some people say the food is poisoned so that people who bring it must eat and drink first.

PAINTER. I was with my girlfriend so I felt I should act as a man and be confident. I was curious to know what I would feel in difficult moments.

STUDENT 1. There are children of 12 or 13 moving everywhere, they are harder to see, bringing us bullets, saying "What do you need? What shall I bring you?"

PAINTER. A man was shot in the throat in front of me. Some people couldn't look but I was staring, trying not to forget. I had an insane curiosity. It was like when they kill an animal. He had an expression of confusedness. It was incredible he had so much blood. I felt empty.

HOUSE PAINTER. At half past eight we leave the TV station to buy some bread, then home to sleep. My mother ask where I was and I say I go out to buy bread, just that.

DOCTOR. On the 23 I went to work. Two boys came in with a young man on a stretcher, which they put down, then one of them fell to the ground and began to scream—

he sees the wounded man is his older brother. His friend takes him down the hall to get a tranquilizer, it is very dark and when they come back the friend trips over something, it is the body of the older brother, who is dead waiting for surgery. The younger brother was only 14. He threw himself on the corpse and won't move, he said he wants to die with his brother.

STUDENT 1. On the morning of the 23 I went home and I slept for two hours. I kept the gun with me in bed.

GIRL STUDENT. I was about to go out to defend my school when my grandmother began to panic and we thought she would have a heart attack, so I promised to stay in, and I spent the day passing messages to people on the phone. Some people don't like me because of my father.

STUDENT 2. The train didn't go that day so I stayed at home. I thought, "This is not my town. I will go to my own town and act there."

DOCTOR. I stayed in the hospital without going home till the 28. We had enough medicine for immediate cases. Once or twice we had to use out of date anaesthetic and the patient woke up during the operation, not often but it happened. We had no coffee or food. When my husband came to see me, more than seeing him I was pleased he had 30 packets of cigarettes. We ate what the patients left and people brought some bread and some jam so on Christmas day we had jam sandwiches.

SECURITATE. When I heard about the execution on the 25 I came at night with my father to the authorities to certify what I was doing during the event. I was detained three days by the army, then told to remain at home. I will say one thing. Until noon on the 22 we were law and order.

We were brought up in this idea. I will never agree with unorder. Everyone looks at me like I did something wrong. It was the way the law was then and the way they all accepted it.

STUDENT 1. On the 25 we hear about the trial and their deaths. It is announced that people must return their weapons so we go to the factory and give back our guns. Of the 28 who had guns only 4 are alive.

BULLDOZER DRIVER. I stay home with my family till the 28, then I go to work. They say the time I was home will be off my vacations. There is no more work on the People's Palace, nobody knows if they finish it.

PAINTER. Painting doesn't mean just describing, it's a state of spirit. I didn't want to paint for a long time then.

III FLORINA'S WEDDING

1. Cîinelui îi e foame. The dog is hungry.

*Night, outside. A DOG is lying asleep. A MAN
approaches. He whistles. The DOG looks up. The man
whistles. The DOG gets up and approaches, undecided
between eagerness and fear. The man is a VAMPIRE.*

VAMPIRE. Good dog. Don't be frightened.

(DOG approaches, then stops. Retreats, advances. Growls.)

VAMPIRE. No no no no no. You can tell of course.
Yes I'm not a human being, what does that matter? It
means you can talk to me.

DOG. Are you dead?

VAMPIRE. No, no I'm not unfortunately. I'm undead
and getting tired of it. I'm a vampire, you may not have
met one before, I usually live in the mountains and you
look like a dog who's lived on scraps in the city. How old
are you?

DOG. Five, six.

VAMPIRE. You look older but that's starvation. I'm
over five hundred but I look younger, I don't go hungry.

DOG. Do you eat dogs?

VAMPIRE. Don't be frightened of me, I'm not hungry
now. And if I was all I'd do is sip a little of your blood, I
don't eat. I don't care for dogs' blood.

DOG. People's blood?

VAMPIRE. I came here for the revolution, I could smell it a long way off.

DOG. I've tasted man's blood. It was thick on the road, I gobbled it up quick, then somebody kicked me.

VAMPIRE. Nobody knew who was doing the killing, I could come up behind a man in a crowd.

DOG. Good times.

VAMPIRE. There's been a lot of good times over the years.

DOG. Not for me.

VAMPIRE. Do you belong to anyone?

DOG. I used to but he threw me out. I miss him. I hate him.

VAMPIRE. He probably couldn't feed you.

DOG. He beat me. But now nobody talks to me.

VAMPIRE. I'm talking to you.

DOG. Will you keep me?

VAMPIRE. No, I'm just passing the time.

DOG. Please. I'm nice. I'm hungry.

VAMPIRE. Vampires don't keep pets.

DOG. You could feed me. (*DOG approaches VAMPIRE carefully.*)

VAMPIRE. I've no money to buy food for you, I don't buy food, I put my mouth to a neck in the night, it's a solitary—get off.

(*As the DOG reaches him he makes a violent gesture and the DOG leaps away.*)

DOG. Don't throw stones at me, I hate it when they throw stones, I hate being kicked, please please I'd be a good dog, I'd bite your enemies. Don't hurt me.

VAMPIRE. I'm not hurting you. Don't get hysterical.

(DOG approaches again.)

DOG. I'm hungry. You're kind. I'm your dog. (*DOG is licking his hand.*)

VAMPIRE. Stop it, go away. Go. Go. Go away.

DOG. (*Slinks a little further off then approaches carefully.*) I'm your dog. Nice. Yes? Your dog? Yes?

VAMPIRE. You want me to make you into a vampire? A vampire dog?

DOG. Yes please, yes yes.

VAMPIRE. It means sleeping all day and going about at night.

DOG. I'd like that.

VAMPIRE. Going about looking like anyone else, being friendly, nobody knowing you.

DOG. I'd like that.

VAMPIRE. Living forever, / you've no idea. All that

DOG. I'd —

VAMPIRE. happens is you begin to want blood, you try to put it off, you're bored with killing, but you can't sit quiet, you can't settle to anything, your limbs ache, your head burns, you have to keep moving faster and faster, that eases the pain, seeking. And finding. Ah.

DOG. I'd like that.

VAMPIRE. And then it's over and you wander round looking for someone to talk to. Every night. Over and over.

DOG. You could talk to me. I could talk to you. I'm your dog.

VAMPIRE. Yes, if you like, I don't mind. Come here. Good dog. (*VAMPIRE puts his mouth to the DOG's neck.*)

3. Toată lumea speră ca Gabriel să se însănătoşească repede. Everyone hopes Gabriel will feel better soon.

i.

GABRIEL is in bed in hospital.
FLORINA, working there as a nurse, passes his bed.

FLORINA. I see less of you working here than if I came for a visit.

GABRIEL. Wait.

FLORINA. I can't.

GABRIEL. We won. Eh? Ole ... Yes?

FLORINA. Yes but don't talk. Wait for your visitors.

GABRIEL. Rodica?

FLORINA. Mom and Dad.

GABRIEL. Something wrong with Rodica?

FLORINA. No.

GABRIEL. You'd tell me / if she was hurt.

FLORINA. Don't talk, Gabriel, rest. She's not hurt.

GABRIEL. Do nurses tell the truth?

FLORINA. I do to you. (*She goes.*)

(*IRINA and BOGDAN arrive with food.*)

IRINA. Eggs in the shops. We're getting the benefit
already. I'll ask Florina who I should give it to. Keep the
apples here. Make sure you get it all, you fought for it.

GABRIEL. Where's Rodica?

IRINA. She couldn't come.

GABRIEL. I want her.

IRINA. Don't, don't you're not well. I'll never forgive
her, she's perfectly all right.

GABRIEL. What?

IRINA. She's frightened to go out. Now when there's
nothing happening. She sends her love.

(BOGDAN has a bottle of whisky.)

BOGDAN. This is for the doctor. / Which doctor

GABRIEL. No need.

BOGDAN. do I give it to?

GABRIEL. No.

IRINA. Yes, a little present for the doctor so he's gentle
with you.

GABRIEL. That was before. Not now.

BOGDAN. When your mother had her operation, two
bottles of whisky and then it was the wrong doctor.

IRINA. They can't change things so quickly, Gaby.

BOGDAN. You do something for somebody, he does
something for you. Won't change that. Give my father a
cigarette, he puts it behind his ear. Because you never
know.

GABRIEL. Different now.

BOGDAN. Who shall I give it to? I'll ask Florina.

*(MIHAI, FLAVIA and RADU arrive. RADU takes
    GABRIEL's hand.)*

MIHAI. Radu wanted to visit his friend Gabriel so we
thought we'd come with him.
    FLAVIA. We've brought a few little things.
    MIHAI. To pay our respects to a hero.

(They stand awkwardly. Then FLAVIA embraces IRINA.)

IRINA. Radu's a hero too.
    FLAVIA. The young show us the way.
    BOGDAN. We're glad you're safe, Radu.
    FLAVIA. And Florina's here?
    IRINA. Yes, she's working.
    MIHAI. You must be proud of her.
    BOGDAN. She worked for five days without stopping.
    RADU. I'll go and find her.
    FLAVIA. Yes, find her, Radu.

(RADU goes.)

MIHAI. We're so glad the young people no longer have
a misunderstanding. We have to put the past behind us and
go forward on a new basis.
    BOGDAN. Yes, nobody can be blamed for what
happened in the past.
    IRINA. Are you warm enough, Gaby? I can bring a
blanket from home.

ii.

Evening in the hospital. Patient(s) in dressing-gown(s).
Someone comes looking for a doctor.

SORE THROAT. I'm looking for the doctor. I have a
sore throat. I need to get an antibiotic.

(A patient shuffles slowly about, taking the person down
corridors and opening doors, looking for a doctor.
Different SOUNDS come from the rooms—a woman
crying, a man muttering (it's the patient from III, we
barely hear what he's saying, just get the sound of
constant questions), a priest chanting. They go off, still
looking.)

iii.

A couple of weeks after i. Sunlight. GABRIEL is much
better, sitting up. RODICA is sitting beside him
holding his hand. Flowers. A PATIENT is a dressing
gown comes to talk to them.

PATIENT. Did we have a revolution or a putsch? Who
was shooting on the 21st? And who was shooting on the
22nd? Was the army shooting on the 21st or did some
shoot and some not shoot or were the Securitate disguised
in army uniforms? If the army were shooting, why haven't
they been brought to justice? And were they still shooting
on the 22nd? Were they now disguised as Securitate? Most
important of all, were the terrorists and the army really
fighting or were they only pretending to fight? And for
whose benefit? And by whose orders? Where did the flags

come from? Who put megaphones in the square? How could they publish a newspaper so soon? Why did no one turn off the power at the TV? Who got Ceauşescu to call everyone together? And is he really dead? How many people died at Timişoara? And where are the bodies? And were they mutilated after they'd been killed specially to provoke a revolution? By whom? For whose benefit? Or was there a drug in the food and water at Timişoara to make people more aggressive? Who poisoned the water in Bucharest?

GABRIEL. Please stop.

PATIENT. Why weren't we shown the film of the execution?

GABRIEL. He is dead.

PATIENT. And is the water still poisoned?

GABRIEL. No.

PATIENT. And who was shooting on the 22nd?

GABRIEL. The army, which was on the side of the people, was fighting the terrorists, who were supporting Ceauşescu.

PATIENT. They changed clothes.

GABRIEL. Who changed clothes?

PATIENT. It was a fancy dress party. Weren't you there? Didn't you see them singing and dancing?

GABRIEL. My sister's coming from America.

PATIENT. Does she know what happened?

GABRIEL. She'll have read the newspapers.

PATIENT. Then you must tell her. Do you know?

GABRIEL. I can't talk about it now.

PATIENT. Are you a Communist?

GABRIEL. No but my sister's / coming now.

PATIENT. Communist. I hope you die.

(FLORINA, RADU and LUCIA.
LUCIA embraces GABRIEL and RODICA.)

LUCIA. All the way over on the plane I was terrified of what I was going to see. But you look beautiful. In America everyone's thrilled. I told my friends, "My brother was there, he was wounded, he's a hero." I watched TV but they never showed enough, I kept playing it and stopping when there was a crowd, I thought I must know somebody, I was crying all the time, I was so ashamed not to be here. I've brought you some chocolate, and oranges.

GABRIEL. How's America?

LUCIA. If you mean how's Wayne he's fine, he's allergic to cats but let's forget that, he has a lot of meetings so he can't be here. But America. There are walls of fruit in America, five different kinds of apples, and oranges, grapes, pears, bananas, melons, different kinds of melon, and things I don't know the name—and the vegetables, the eggplants are a purple they look as if they've been varnished, red, yellow, green, peppers, white onions, red onions, bright orange carrots somebody has shined every carrot. I still stare every time I go shopping. And the garbage, everyone throws away big bags full of food and paper and cans, every day, huge bags, huge trash cans, people live out of them. Eat some chocolate.

(They eat the chocolate.
PATIENT comes back again.)

PATIENT. Have they told you who was shooting on the 22nd? / And why was it necessary to kill

GABRIEL. Please, not now.

PATIENT. Ceausescu so quickly?

LUCIA. Have some chocolate.

PATIENT. (*Takes some chocolate and puts it in his pocket.*) Who has taken the supplies we were sent from the west? Nurse?

FLORINA. I'm not on duty.

PATIENT. Did we have a revolution? Or what did we have?

RADU. Come on, let's find your bed. (*RADU takes him off still talking.*)

PATIENT. Why did they close the schools a week early? Why did they evacuate the foreigners from the geriatric hospital? Who were the men in blue suits who appeared on the streets before the 21st?

(*Silence.*)

LUCIA. They have mental patients in here with the wounded? That's not very good.

FLORINA. He was wounded on the head. / He has

LUCIA. That explains a lot.

FLORINA. headaches and gets upset. Yes, he's a bit crazy.

(*Pause.*)

LUCIA. Hungarians were fighting beside us they said on TV. And Ianos wasn't hurt, that's good. I think Americans like Hungarians.

GABRIEL. The poor Hungarians have a bad time because they're not treated better than everyone else. How did they treat us when they had the chance? They go abroad and insult Romania to make people despise us.

LUCIA. This is what we used to say before. Don't we say something different?

GABRIEL. Ask Granny about Hungarians.

LUCIA. It's true, in America they even like the idea of gypsies, they think how quaint. But I said to them you don't like blacks here, you don't like hispanics, we're talking about lazy greedy crazy people who drink too much and get rich on the black market. That shut them up.

GABRIEL. But Ianos doesn't count as Hungarian.

(RADU comes back.)

LUCIA. So you got rid of the lunatic all right? Have some more chocolate.

(RADU shakes his head.)

LUCIA. Go on, there's plenty more.

RADU. We're not greedy, Lucia. We don't just think about food.

LUCIA. It's a celebration, it's fun to have chocolate, can't you have fun?

RADU. No I can't. Celebrate what?

FLORINA. Radu, not now.

RADU. Who was shooting on the 22nd? That's not a crazy question.

FLORINA. Lucia's just arrived. Gabriel's still not well.

RADU. The only real night was the 21st. After that, what was going on? It was all a show.

LUCIA. No, it was real, Radu / I saw it on television.

FLORINA. I don't want to hear / all this now.

RADU. Were they fighting or pretending to fight? Who set off firecrackers? Who brought megaphones?

(Pause.
LUCIA looks at FLORINA.)

FLORINA. At the Municipal Hospital the head doctor gave medical supplies from the west to the police to sell on the black market. / And he locked the wounded in

LUCIA. That I can believe.

RADU. a room with no one to take care of them so he could hand them over / to the Securitate and some of them died.

LUCIA. But that's just him. It's not a plot.

(Pause.)

FLORINA. How many people were killed at Timişoara? Where are the bodies? There were bodies found in a sandpit for the long jump. / Where are the rest?

LUCIA. But what does that mean?

RADU. Why did no one turn off the power at the TV station?

(Pause.)

LUCIA. Gabriel? Rodica?

GABRIEL. I'm too tired.

(RODICA turns her head away.)

i v .

Some time later. IRINA helping GABRIEL to walk. He
reaches a chair and falls into it laughing.

IRINA. Good. Good.

(Silence.)

IRINA. I used to say more with the radio on.
GABRIEL. Have you heard people say that by the 22nd
/ the revolution had been stolen?
IRINA. No no no no no. I've no time for all that
nonsense.
GABRIEL. But—
IRINA. No. No no no. Now. Walk.

3. Rodica mai are coşmare. Rodica is still
having nightmares.

RODICA is wearing a cloak and a big fur hat with dollars
and flowers on it. Two soldiers come in.

SOLDIER 1. We're the last soldiers, your Majesty. The
rest of the army's on the side of the people.
SOLDIER 2. The helicopter's going to rescue you.

(She takes a telephone from under her cloak and dials
endlessly.

*The SOLDIERS take off their uniforms and get dressed
again in each other's identical clothes. Meanwhile
GABRIEL comes in wearing a huge Romanian flag, his
head through the hole. He gives RODICA a box of
matches and goes.*

SOLDIER 2. Why doesn't anyone love you after all
you've done for them?
SOLDIER 1. Have you enough money to pay for the
helicopter?

*(She gives them money from her hat. They pocket each
thing she gives them and hold out their hands for more
till she has nothing left on her hat. She gives them the
hat. They hold out their hands for more.)*

SOLDIER 1. Give us your hands.

(Her hands disappear under her cloak.)

SOLDIER 2. Give us your feet.

*(Her feet disappear under her cloak and she sinks down till
she is kneeling.)*

SOLDIER 1. There's no helicopter. You'll have to run.

*(The SOLDIERS go.
RODICA opens the matchbox—"ole ole ole ole" chanted
by a huge crowd. She opens and closes it several times
and the song continues each time. Sound of gunfire.*

She looks round in a panic for somewhere to hide the
  matchbox—which she swallows.
A SOLDIER comes in and searches, kicking at anything in
  the way.
He goes to her and opens her mouth.
"Ole ole ole ole" chanted by huge crowd.
He opens and closes her mouth several times, the chant
  continues each time.)

**4. Cind am fost să ne vizităm bunicii la
ţară, era o zi însorită. When we went to visit
our grandparents in the country it was a sunny
day.**

FLORINA, LUCIA, RADU and IANOŞ are visiting
  FLORINA and LUCIA's GRANDPARENTS in the
  country, so they can meet RADU before the wedding.
  The GRANDPARENTS are peasants. IANOŞ has a
  child with him, a boy of about 8, TOMA. The
  following things happen in the course of a long sunny
  afternoon, out of doors, immediately outside the
  GRANDPARENTS' house where there is a bench, and
  nearby.

i.
The GRANDPARENTS embrace LUCIA and FLORINA,
  greet RADU warmly, IANOŞ more formally. TOMA
  clings shyly to IANOŞ.

ii.

IANOŞ has a ball and tries to interest TOMA in playing with him and RADU. They go off.

RADU. Toma! Ianos!
GRANDMOTHER. That young man's a Hungarian.
LUCIA. He's a friend of Radu and Gabriel's, Granny.
GRANDMOTHER. I knew a woman married a Hungarian. His brother killed her and ripped the child out of her stomach.
FLORINA. He's just a friend of Gabriel's, Granny.
GRANDMOTHER. Radu seems a nice young man. He's Romanian. What's wrong with that child?
FLORINA. He's been in an orphanage.
GRANDMOTHER. Is it a gypsy?
LUCIA. Of course not.
GRANDMOTHER. They wouldn't let him adopt a Romanian.

.

iii.

LUCIA with IANOŞ and TOMA.

LUCIA. Do we have to have him with us all the time?
IANOŞ. He likes me.
LUCIA. I like you but I'm not getting much chance to show it.
IANOŞ. He'll settle down.
LUCIA. Can he talk?
IANOŞ. Yes of course.
LUCIA. I haven't heard him.
IANOŞ. He doesn't know you.

LUCIA. I think your parents are remarkable. What if it goes wrong? Can you give him back?

IANOȘ. We don't want to give him back. We're adopting him.

LUCIA. Your parents are adopting him.

IANOȘ. Yes but me too.

LUCIA. (*Rolls the ball.*) Don't you want to play with the ball, Toma? (*She goes and gets it herself.*) Ball. Ball. Can you say ball, Toma?

(*TOMA buries himself in IANOȘ.*)

LUCIA. I think your parents are sentimental.

IANOS. Are you going back to America?

(*LUCIA shrugs.*)

IANOȘ. I still owe your husband money.

LUCIA. Did you borrow money from him?

IANOȘ. He paid for the abortion.

LUCIA. But he didn't know. It was money he gave me, it was my money. You can't pay him back, he'd want to know what it was for.

IANOȘ. I haven't got the money anyway.

(*Pause.*)

IANOȘ. Aren't you ashamed?

LUCIA. Of what? No.

IANOȘ. Not the abortion.

LUCIA. What?

IANOȘ. I don't know. The wedding?

LUCIA. No, why?
IANOŞ. I'm ashamed.
LUCIA. Why?

(Pause.)

IANOŞ. I'm ashamed of loving you when I think you're probably not very nice.

(Silence.)

LUCIA. Shall I stay here and marry you?

(Silence.)

LUCIA. This is the last of the chocolate.

*(As she gets it out, TOMA pounces on it and runs a little
      way off, stuffing it all into his mouth.)*

LUCIA. You horrible child. I hate you.
IANOŞ. Don't shout at him. How can he help it?
You're so stupid.
LUCIA. Don't shout at me.

*(TOMA whimpers. He starts to shake his head
      obsessively.)*

IANOŞ. Toma. Come here.

*(TOMA goes on.
IANOS goes to him.)*

IANOŞ. Toma.

*(TOMA hits IANOŞ and starts to bellow with panic.
IANOŞ holds him, he subsides into whimpering.
IANOŞ sits on the ground holding him.)*

LUCIA. Did you tell anyone about us after I left?
IANOŞ. No.
LUCIA. It might be better if we're seen as something
new.

(Silence.)

LUCIA. Is he very difficult?
IANOŞ. Not yet. Most of the time he's so good it's
frightening. The babies there don't cry.
LUCIA. He's going to be terrible. I won't be much use.

(Silence.)

IANOŞ. I'd like to go to America. I've got a passport.
LUCIA. Just for a vacation. I don't like America.
IANOŞ. So is that the only reason you want to stay
here? I hoped you loved America. *(Pause.)* Would your
family let you marry a Hungarian?

iv.
RADU and FLORINA. RADU drawing.

RADU. Iliescu's going to get in because the workers and peasants are stupid. (*Pause.*) Not stupid but they don't think. They don't have the information. (*Pause.*) I don't mean your family in particular.

FLORINA. You're a snob like your father. You'd have joined the party.

RADU. Wouldn't you? (*Silence. He touches her face.*)

FLORINA. I used to feel free then.

RADU. You can't have.

FLORINA. I don't now and I'm in a panic.

RADU. It's because the Front tricked us. / When we've got rid—

FLORINA. It's because I could keep everything out.

(*Pause.*)

RADU. But you didn't have me then.

FLORINA. No but I thought you were perfect.

RADU. I am perfect.

(*Silence.*)

RADU. What?

FLORINA. Sometimes I miss him.

RADU. What? Why?

FLORINA. I miss him.

RADU. You miss hating him.

FLORINA. Maybe it's that.

RADU. I hate Iliescu.

FLORINA. That's not the same.

RADU. I hate him worse. Human face. And he'll get in because they're stupid and do what they're told. Ceausescu Ceausescu, Iliescu, Iliescu.

FLORINA. I don't have anyone to hate. You sometimes.

RADU. Me?

FLORINA. Not really.

RADU. Me?

v.

The GRANDPARENTS are sitting side by side on the bench, the others around them. The GRANDPARENTS speak slowly, the others fast.

GRANDFATHER. He was killed while he was putting up posters.

RADU. You see? they're murderers. / It's the same

LUCIA. For which party, Grandpa?

RADU. tactics / of intimidation.

IANOȘ. Who killed him?

GRANDFATHER. Posters for the Peasants Party.

FLORINA. Is that / who you support?

RADU. The Front claim the country supports them but it's only / because of intimidation.

IANOȘ. So did they find out who killed him?

GRANDMOTHER. Yes, it was gypsies killed him.

RADU. Gypsies? / They were probably paid by the

FLORINA. How did they know it was them?

RADU. Front.

IANOȘ. They'd hardly need paying to murder somebody.

RADU. Or it could have been Front supporters /

LUCIA. Or Securitate.

RADU. and they put the blame on the gypsies.

GRANDFATHER. It was two gypsies, a father and son, who used to work in his garden. They had a quarrel with him. He used to beat them.

LUCIA. So was it just a quarrel, / not politics at all?

FLORINA. Did anyone see them?

GRANDMOTHER. But that quarrel was years ago.

GRANDFATHER. A lot of people didn't like him because he used to be a big landowner. The Peasants Party would give him back his land.

FLORINA. So was he killed because / the rest of the

LUCIA. I thought the Peasants Party was for peasants.

IANOȘ. No, they're millionaires the leaders of it.

FLORINA. village didn't want him to get all the land?

LUCIA. He should get it / if it's his.

FLORINA. No after all this time working on it / everyone—

RADU. Never mind that, he was against the Front, that's why they killed him. He was against the Communists.

GRANDFATHER. He was a party member. He was very big round here. He was a big Securitate man.

LUCIA. So whose side was he on?

GRANDMOTHER. He wasn't a nice man. Nobody liked him.

vi.

*GRANDFATHER is sitting on the bench, the others lying
on the grass, each separately except that TOMA is near
IANOŞ. Long silence.*

IANOŞ. I want to go to Peru.
RADU. Rome. And Pompeii.
LUCIA. A vacation by the sea.

(Pause.)

FLORINA. Sleep late in the morning.

(Pause.)

RADU. Paint what I see in my head.
FLORINA. Go into work tomorrow and everyone's
better.
LUCIA. Gabriel walking.
IANOŞ. Rodica talking.

(They laugh.)

FLORINA. New shoes.
RADU. Paintbrushes with fine points.

(Pause.)

FLORINA. Drive a fast car.
LUCIA. Be famous.
IANOŞ. Toblerone.

(Pause.)

RADU. Make money.

(Pause.)

IANOȘ. Learn everything in the world by the end of the week.

(Pause.)

LUCIA. Not be frightened.

(The pauses get longer.)

RADU. Make Florina happy.

(Long pause.)

IANOȘ. Make Toma happy.

(Silence.)

FLORINA. Live forever.

(Longer silence.)

LUCIA. Die young.

(Very long silence.)

FLORINA. Go on lying here.

(Very long silence.)

5. Mai doreşti puţină brînză? Would you like some more cheese?

MIHAI and FLAVIA eating cheese and salami.

FLAVIA. You know when Radu was born and they said he'd be born dead. Three days, no hope. And then Radu. The pain stops just like that. And then joy. I felt the same the morning of the 22nd. Did you ever feel joy before?

MIHAI. I'm not sure I did.

FLAVIA. All those years of pain forgotten. You felt that?

MIHAI. It was certainly a remarkable experience.

FLAVIA. It can't last of course. Three days after he was born I was crying. But I still loved Radu. And what have we still got from the 22nd?

MIHAI. The work on the People's Palace will probably continue as soon as its new function has been determined.

FLAVIA. What?

MIHAI. If not I'm sure they'll find me some other work. I'm not in any way compromised, I was on the streets, I'm clearly a supporter of the Front. And in any case—

FLAVIA. I wasn't talking about you.

MIHAI. Good, I had the impression you might be worried.

(Pause.)

FLAVIA. All I was trying to do was teach correctly. Isn't history what's in the history book? Let them give me a new book. I'll teach that.

MIHAI. Are you losing your job?

FLAVIA. I didn't inform on my pupils, I didn't accept bribes. Those are the people whose names should be on the list.

MIHAI. Are they not on the list?

FLAVIA. They are on the list but why am I with them? The new head of the department doesn't like me. He knows I'm a better teacher than he is. I can't stop teaching, I'll miss the children.

(Silence during which RADU comes in.)

FLAVIA. Why are you always out, Radu? Come and eat.

(RADU is already making sandwiches.)

MIHAI. I hope you're going to join us for a meal, Radu.

RADU. *(Goes on making sandwiches.)* Have you noticed the way Iliescu moves his hands? And the words he uses?

MIHAI. He comes from a period when that was the style.

RADU. Yes, he does, doesn't he.

MIHAI. Not tonight, Radu. Your mother's had bad news at work about her job.

FLAVIA. The new head of the department.

RADU. There you are. It's because of me. No one who's opposed to the Front / will get anywhere.

MIHAI. Radu, I don't know what to do with you. Nothing is on a realistic basis.

RADU. Please don't say that.

MIHAI. What's the matter now?

RADU. Don't say "realistic basis."

FLAVIA. It's true, Mihai, you do talk in terrible jargon from before, it's no longer correct.

MIHAI. The head of the department is in fact a supporter of the Liberals.

RADU. Is he?

FLAVIA. It may not come to anything.

RADU. You mean it's because of what you did before? What did you do?

MIHAI. Radu, this is not a constructive approach.

RADU. It won't come to anything, don't worry. It's been five weeks since we made our list of bad teachers. Nobody cares that the students and staff voted. It has to go to the Ministry.

FLAVIA. Do you want me to lose my job?

RADU. If you deserve to.

(FLAVIA slaps RADU.
Silence.)

RADU. Do you remember once I came home from school and asked if you loved Elena Ceauşescu?

FLAVIA. I don't remember, no. When was that?

RADU. And you said yes. I was seven.

FLAVIA. No, I don't remember. (*Pause.*) But you can
see now why somebody would say what they had to say to
protect you.

RADU. I've always remembered that.

FLAVIA. I don't remember.

RADU. No, you wouldn't.

(*Pause.*)

FLAVIA. Why are you saying this, Radu? Are you
making it up? You're manipulating me to make me feel
bad. I told you the truth about plenty of things.

RADU. I don't remember.

FLAVIA. No, you wouldn't. (*Silence.*) Now. We have
some dried apples.

RADU. I expect Dad got them from someone with a
human face. (*RADU is about to leave.*)

MIHAI. Radu, how do you think you got into the Art
Institute?

RADU. The still life with the green vase was the one /
they particularly—

MIHAI. Yes your work was all right. I couldn't have
managed if it was below average.

(*RADU leaves MIHAI with the sandwiches and goes.
Silence.*)

MIHAI. Who do we know who can put in a word for
you?

FLAVIA. We don't know who we know. Someone who
put in a word before may be just the person to try and keep
clear of. (*Pause.*) But Radu's painting is exceptional.

MIHAI. Yes, in fact I didn't do anything.
FLAVIA. You must tell him.
MIHAI. He won't believe me.

(Pause.)

FLAVIA. Twenty years marching in the wrong
direction. I'd as soon stop. Twenty years' experience and
I'm a beginner. Yes, stop. There, I feel better. I'm not a
teacher.
MIHAI. They might just transfer you to the provinces.
(Pause.) It won't happen. Trust me. *(Silence. MIHAI goes
on with his meal.)*
FLAVIA. Granny. Granny?

*(Her GRANDMOTHER doesn't come. Silence.
FLAVIA goes on with her meal.)*

**6. Gabriel vine acasă diseară. Gabriel is
coming home tonight.**

*Downstairs in the block of flats where GABRIEL and
    RODICA live. GABRIEL, with a crutch, is arriving
    home from hospital with RADU, FLORINA, LUCIA,
    IANOŞ and other friends. They have been for a drink on
    the way and have some bottles with them.*

ALL.
The elevator's broken.
How do we get Gaby up the stairs?

We'll have the party here.
Rodica's waiting in the apartment.
We shouldn't have stayed so long at the Berlin.
We can carry him up.
We need a drink first.
Let's do it here.
Do it, I've never seen it.
Yes, Radu, to celebrate Gaby coming home.

(Someone announces:)

The trial and execution of Nicolae and Elena Ceauşescu.

(RADU and FLORINA are the Ceausescus.)

IANOŞ. Hurry up. Move along.
RADU. Where are they taking us, Elena?
FLORINA. I don't know, Nicu. He's a very rude man.
RADU. Don't worry we'll be rescued in a minute. This
is all part of my long-term plan.

*(CEAUSEŞCU [RADU] keeps looking at his watch and up
at the sky.)*

IANOŞ. Sit down.
FLORINA. Don't sit down.
RADU. My legs are tired.
FLORINA. Stand up.
IANOŞ. Sit down.
RADU. The Securitate will get in touch with my
watch.
IANOŞ. Answer the questions of the court.

RADU. What court? I don't see any court. Do you, Elena?

FLORINA. No court anywhere here.

RADU. The only judges I recognise are ones I've appointed myself.

SOMEONE. You're on trial for genocide.

FLORINA. These people are hooligans. They're in the pay of foreign powers. That one's just come back from America.

ALL.

Who gave the order to shoot at Timişoara?

What did you have for dinner last night?

Why have you got gold faucets in bathroom?

Do you shit in a gold toilet?

Shitting bricks now.

Why did you tear down my uncle's house?

Etc.

FLORINA. Where's the helicopter?

RADU. On its way.

FLORINA. Have these people arrested and mutilated.

RADU. Maybe just arrested and shot. They are our children.

FLORINA. After all we've done for them. You should kiss my hand. You should drink my bathwater.

ALL.

That's enough trial.

We find you guilty on all counts.

Execution now.

FLORINA. You said there'd be a helicopter, Nicu.

IANOS. Stand up.

FLORINA. Sit down.

(They are roughly pushed to another place.)

RADU. You can't shoot me. I'm the one who gives the orders to shoot.
FLORINA. We don't recognise being shot.
ALL.
Gypsy.
Murderer.
Illiterate.
We've all fucked your wife.
We're fucking her now.
Let her have it.

(They all shoot ELENA [FLORINA], who falls dead at once. GABRIEL, who is particularly vicious throughout this, shoots with his crutch. All make gun noises, then cheer. CEAUSEŞCU [RADU] runs back and forth. They shout again.)

ALL.
We fucked your wife.
Your turn now.
Murderer.
Bite your throat out.

(Meanwhile CEAUSEŞCU [RADU] is pleading.)

RADU. Not me, you've shot her that's enough, I've money in Switzerland, I'll give you the number of my bank account, you can go and get my money—
IANOŞ. In his legs.

(They shoot and he falls over, still talking and crawling about.)

RADU. My helicopter's coming, you'll be sorry, let me go to Iran—
    IANOŞ. In the belly.

(They shoot, he collapses further but keeps talking.)

RADU. I'll give you the People's Palace—
IANOS. In the head.

(They shoot again. He lies still.
They all cheer and jeer.
CEAUSEŞCU [RADU] sits up.)

RADU. But am I dead?
ALL. Yes.

(He falls dead again.
More cheering, ole ole ole etc.
RADU and FLORINA get up, everyone's laughing.
IANOŞ hugs LUCIA lightly.
GABRIEL suddenly hits out at IANOS with his crutch.)

GABRIEL. Get your filthy Hungarian hands off her.
IANOŞ. What?
GABRIEL. Just joking?

(A MAN looks out of one of the doors of the flats to see what the noise is. They go quiet. He shuts the door.)

**7. Abia terminase lucrul, cind a venit Radu.
She had just finished work when Radu came.**

*Hospital at night. A corridor. FLORINA has just come off
duty. RADU is meeting her. They hug.*

FLORINA. Someone died tonight. It was his fifth
operation. When they brought him in all the nurses were in
love with him. But he looked like an old man by the time
he died.

RADU. Was he one of the ones shot low in the back
and out through the shoulder?

FLORINA. He was shot from above in the shoulder and
it came out down low in his back.

RADU. No, all those wounds are / from being—

FLORINA. You don't know anything about it. I was
nursing him.

RADU. A doctor told me.

FLORINA. What does it matter? / He's dead anyway.

RADU. They were in the crowd with us shooting
people in the back. (*Pause.*) And where are they now?

(*Pause.*)

FLORINA. So what have you done today? Sat in the
square and talked?

RADU. I know you're tired.

FLORINA. I like being tired, I like working, I don't
like listening to you talk.

RADU. People are talking about a hunger strike.
FLORINA. Fine, those of you who weren't killed can kill yourselves.

(Pause.)

RADU. Do you want to know what it's for?
FLORINA. No. (*Pause.*) I hope you're not thinking of it.
RADU. Someone's been getting to you, haven't they?
FLORINA. Because if you do / the wedding's off.
RADU. Someone's threatened you. Or offered you something.
FLORINA. It's what I think. / Did you really say that?
RADU. I don't like what you think.
FLORINA. I don't like what you think. You just want to go on playing hero, / you're weak, you're lazy—
RADU. You're betraying the dead. Aren't you ashamed? Yes, I'm a hooligan. Let's forget we know each other. / Communist.
FLORINA. You don't know me.

(RADU goes.
FLORINA is alone.
She is joined by the GHOST of a young man.)

GHOST. I'm dead and I never got married. So I've come to find somebody. I was always looking at you when I was sick. But you loved Radu then. I won't talk like he does. I died, that's all I want to know about it. Please love me. It's lonely when you're dead. I have to go down a secret road. Come with me. It's simple.

8. Multǎ fericire. We wish you happiness.

FLORINA and RADU's wedding party at a hotel. Both
families are there, and old peasant AUNT of Bogdan's
and a WAITER. MUSIC in background. The following
conversations take place, sometimes overlapping or
simultaneously.

1.
FLAVIA. What's so wonderful about a wedding is
everyone laughs and cries and it's like the revolution again.
Because everyone's gone back behind their masks. Don't
you think so?
BOGDAN. I don't know. Perhaps. You could say that.

2.
MIHAI. I forgot to take my windshield wipers off last
night so of course they've been stolen. Still, my son
doesn't get married every day.

3.
IRINA. She and her followers talk without speaking,
they know each other's thoughts. She just looks at you and
she knows your troubles. I told her all about Gaby.
LUCIA. So you told her your troubles. No wonder she
knows.
IRINA. When they send him to Italy for his operation
maybe we won't need a psychic. She said I could take him
to see her.

LUCIA. He'll just laugh.

IRINA. She says we have no soul. We've suffered for so many years and we don't know how to live. Are people very different in other countries, Lucia?

LUCIA. Cheer up, have a drink. It's Florina's wedding day.

IRINA. I'll miss Florina.

4.

LUCIA is talking to a smiling WAITER.

WAITER. I remember your wedding last year. That was a very different time. We had bugs in the vases. Still. Can I help you change some dollars?

LUCIA. No thank you.

WAITER. I used to help your husband. It's easier now. My brother's gone to Switzerland to buy a Mercedes. You're sure I can't help you? Top rate, high as Everest.

LUCIA. Thank you but I don't have any dollars left.

(The WAITER's smile disappears.)

5.

BOGDAN. I know someone at work killed his son-in-law. He put an axe in his head. Then he put a knife in the dead man's hand to make like it was self-defense, and said anyway he wasn't there, it was his son. And he got away with it. Smart, huh?

RADU. What happened to the son?

BOGDAN. Luckily he had some money, he only got six years.

RADU. What's he going to do to his dad when he gets out?

(They laugh.)

6.
FLAVIA. How's your little brother?
IANOS. He wakes up in the night now and cries.
FLAVIA. How's your mother.

(They laugh.)

7.
FLORINA. I thought I was going to get the giggles.
RADU. It was good though.
FLORINA. It was lovely.

8.
IANOS. Lucia and I are going to start a newspaper.
LUCIA. A friend's sending us magazines from America and we'll translate interesting articles.
IANOS. *(To LUCIA.)* Do people really dress like in *Vogue*?

9.
IRINA. I bought these shoes in the street.
FLAVIA. Did they want dollars?
IRINA. Yes, Lucia's last dollars were spent on the wedding.
FLAVIA. Black market prices have shot up.
IRINA. It's not black market, it's free market.

10.

IANOS. A French doctor told me 4000 babies / have it.

GABRIEL. I hate the French, they're so superior.

IANOS. Yes, they do like to help.

GABRIEL. Merci, merci.

IANOS. Can you really sterilise infected needles with alcohol?

GABRIEL. I'm sterilising myself with alcohol.

11.

Old peasant AUNT shouts ritual chants at FLORINA.

AUNT.
Little bride, little bride,
You're laughing, we've cried.
Now a man's come to choose you
We're sad because we lose you.
Makes you proud to be a wife
But it's not an easy life.
Your husband isn't like a brother
Your mother-in-law's not like a mother.
More fun running free and wild
Than staying home to mind a child.
Better to be on the shelf
Only have to please yourself.
Little bride don't be sad,
Not to marry would be mad.
Single girls are all in tears,
They'll be lonely many years.
Lovely girl you're like a flower, /
Only pretty for an hour—

BOGDAN. Stop it, Auntie, you're not on the farm now.

FLORINA. No, I like it. Go on.

(By now people have had more to drink, begin to be more cheerful, emotion, aggressive.)

1.

IRINA. If only he'd stayed in University Square.

LUCIA. He could have been shot there.

IRINA. The bullets missed Ianos.

LUCIA. Do you wish they'd hit him?

IRINA. No but of course anyone else.

2.

FLORINA. Be nice to your mom and dad.

RADU. I am nice.

3.

BOGDAN. Bitch, bitch. Gaby was shot, all right. Everyone bitches. Layabout students. Radu and Ianos never stop talking, want to smack them in the mouth. "Was it a revolution?" Of course it was. / My son was shot for it and we've got

MIHAI. Certainly. Of course.

BOGDAN. This country needs a strong man.

MIHAI. And we've got one.

BOGDAN. We've got one. Iliescu's a strong man. We can't have a traffic jam forever. Are they going to clear the square or not?

MIHAI. The government has to avoid any action that would give credibility to the current unsubstantiated allegations.

BOGDAN. They're weak, aren't they.

4.

FLAVIA. I'm going to write a true history, Florina, so we'll know exactly what happened. How much do you think Moscow was involved / in planning the coup?

FLORINA. I don't know. I don't care. I'm sorry.

FLAVIA. What did you vote? Liberal?

FLORINA. Yes of course.

FLAVIA. So did I, so did I. (*She hugs FLORINA.*) Mihai doesn't know. And next time we'll win. Jos Iliescu.

5.

RADU. Look at Gaby, crippled for nothing. They've voted the same bunch in.

IRINA. It's thanks to Gaby you can talk like this.

6.

JANOŞ. Have another drink.

LUCIA. I've had another drink.

JANOŞ. Have another other drink.

(They laugh.)

7.

IRINA. Ceauşescu shouldn't have been shot.

RADU. Because he would have exposed people / in the Front.

IRINA. He should have been hung up in a cage and stones thrown at him.

(They laugh.)

8.
BOGDAN. *(To MIHAI.)* If Radu had been hurt instead of Gaby, he'd be in that hospital in Italy by now.

9.
GABRIEL. I can't work. Rodica can't work. What's going to happen to us? I wish I'd been killed.
FLORINA. You're going to Italy.
GABRIEL. When? Can't you do something to hurry things up, Florina? Sleep with a doctor? Just joking.

10.
IRINA. I don't like seeing you with Ianos.
LUCIA. He's Gabriel's friend.
IRINA. I was once in a shop in Transylvania and they wouldn't serve me because I couldn't speak Hungarian. / In my own country.
LUCIA. Yes, but—
IRINA. And what if the doctor only spoke Hungarian / and someone wanted a doctor?
BOGDAN. Stuck-up bastards.
IRINA. Are you going back to America? You're not going back.
LUCIA. Didn't you miss me?
IRINA. Aren't you ashamed? Two years of hell to get your precious American and you don't even want him. Did he beat you?

LUCIA. I got homesick.

IRINA. Was Ianos going on before?

LUCIA. Of course not. You didn't think that?

IRINA. I don't know what I thought. I just made the wedding dress.

LUCIA. You like Ianos.

IRINA. Go back to America, Lucia, and maybe we can all go. You owe us that.

BOGDAN. You're a slut, Lucia.

11.

FLAVIA. Where are the tapes they made when they listened to everyone talking? All that history wasted. I'd like to find someone in the Securitate who could tell me. Bogdan, do you know anyone?

BOGDAN. Why me?

FLAVIA. I used to know someone but she's disappeared.

BOGDAN. They should be driven into the open and punished. Big public trials. The Front aren't doing their job.

FLAVIA. There wouldn't be enough prisons.

BOGDAN. (*To MIHAI.*) There's a use for your People's Palace.

12.

MIHAI. I was in the British Embassy library reading the Architect's Journal and there's a building in Japan forty stories high with a central atrium up to twenty stories. So the problem is how to get light into the central volume. The German engineer has an ingenious solution where they've installed computerised mirrors angled to follow the sun so they reflect natural light into the atrium according to the season and the time of day, so you have sunlight in a completely enclosed space.

13.
FLORINA. I'm glad about you and Ianoş. (*They kiss.*) Tell me something.

LUCIA. Don't ask.

FLORINA. No, tell me.

LUCIA. Two years is a long time when you hardly know somebody. I'd lost my job, I had to go through with it, I wanted to get away.

FLORINA. But you loved Wayne at first? If you didn't I'll kill you.

LUCIA. Of course I did. But don't tell Ianos.

14.
PRIEST. You can't blame anybody. Everyone was trying to survive.

BOGDAN. Wipe them out. Even if it's the entire population. We're garbage. The Front are stuck-up bastards. They'd have to wipe themselves out too.

PRIEST. We have to try to love our enemies.

BOGDAN. Plenty of enemies. So we must be the most loving people in the world. Did you love him? Give him a kiss would you?

PRIEST. When I say love. It's enough not to hate.

BOGDAN. Handy for you having God say be nice to Ceauşescu.

PRIEST. You're your own worst enemy, Bogdan.

BOGDAN. So I ought to love myself best.

PRIEST. Don't hate yourself anyway.

BOGDAN. Why not? Don't you? You're a smug fuck.

(Two simultaneous conversations develop so that there are two distinct groups. Everyone has drunk a lot by now. BOGDAN, who is too drunk to care if anyone listens, puts remarks at random to either group.)

1.

BOGDAN.

a. Private schools, private hospitals. I've seen what happens to old people. I want to buy my father a decent death.

b. I support the Peasants Party because my father's a peasant. I'm not ashamed of that. They should have their land because their feet are in the earth and they know things nobody else knows. Birds, frogs, cows, god, the direction of the wind.

c. CIA, KGB, we're all in the hands of foreign agents. That's one point where I'm right behind Ceauşescu.

2.

MIHAI, RADU and FLORINA, joined by FLAVIA.

MIHAI. The front wouldn't fix the vote because they knew they were going to win. Everyone appreciates the sacrifice made by youth. The revolution is in safe hands. This isn't a day for worrying, Florina and Radu, you take too much on. I wish you could let it all go for a little while. Please believe me, I want your happiness.

FLORINA. We know you do. *(She kisses him.)*

RADU. Yes, I know. I appreciate that.

MIHAI. After all, I'm not a monster. Most of the country supports the Front. It's only in my own home it takes courage to say it. We have a government of reconciliation.

FLAVIA. Why don't the Front tell the truth and admit they're communists? / * nothing to be

MIHAI. Because they're not.

RADU. * I don't care what they're called, it's the same people.

FLAVIA. ashamed of in communism, / nothing to be

FLORINA. They should have been banned / from

MIHAI. That's your idea of freedom, banning people?

FLORINA. running in the election.

RADU. We've got to have another revolution.

FLAVIA. ashamed of in planning the revolution if they'd just admit it. You never dared speak out against Ceausescu, Mihai, and you don't dare speak out now. Say it, I'm a communist and so what. / Say it, I'm a communist.

RADU. Jos comunismul, jos comunismul. / Jos Iliescu. Jos tiranul. Jos Iliescu. Jos Iliescu.

FLORINA. Radu, don't be childish.

(BOGDAN joins in shouting "Jos comunismul," then turns his attention to the other group.)

3.

GABRIEL, at first in group with MIHAI then with LUCIA, IANOŞ and IRINA.

GABRIEL. The only reason we need an internal security force is if Hungary tried to invade us / we'd need to be sure—

LUCIA. Invade? are you serious?

IANOȘ. When we get Transylvania back it's going to be legally / because it's ours.

IRINA. You're not going to marry a Hungarian.

LUCIA. I'm married already.

IANOȘ. Gaby, the Hungarians started the revolution. Without us you'd still be worshipping Ceausescu. / And

(GABRIEL jeers.)

LUCIA. We didn't worship him.

IRINA. Gaby's a hero, Ianos.

IANOȘ. now the Romanians worship Iliescu. Who's the opposition? Hungarians.

GABRIEL. That's just voting for your language.

LUCIA. Why shouldn't they have their own schools?

IRINA. And lock Romanian children out in the street. If it wasn't bad enough you going to America, now a Hungarian, / and Gaby crippled, and Radu's irresponsible, I worry for Florina.

GABRIEL. If they want to live in Romania / they can

LUCIA. In the riots on TV I saw a Hungarian on the

GABRIEL. speak Romanian.

IANOȘ. We can learn two languages, we're not stupid.

LUCIA. ground and Romanians kicking him.

GABRIEL. That was a Romanian on the ground, and Hungarians—you think we're stupid?

IANOȘ. You were under the Turks too long, it made you like slaves.

LUCIA. You think I'm a slave? I'm not your slave.

(*GABRIEL pushes IANOŞ, who pushes him back.*
BOGDAN arrives.)

BOGDAN. Leave my son alone. Hungarian bastard.
And don't come near my daughter.
IANOŞ. I'm already fucking your daughter, you stupid
peasant. *Oh yikes*

(*BOGDAN hits IANOŞ.*
RADU restrains BOGDAN.
LUCIA attacks BOGDAN.
BOGDAN hits RADU.
MIHAI pushes BOGDAN.
BOGDAN hits MIHAI.
FLAVIA attacks BOGDAN.
IANOŞ pushes GABRIEL.
IRINA protects GABRIEL.
GABRIEL hits IANOS.
RADU attacks BOGDAN.
MIHAI restrains RADU.
RADU attacks MIHAI.
FLORINA attacks RADU.
GABRIEL hits out indiscriminately with his crutch and
    accidentally knocks BOGDAN to the floor.
Stunned silence.)

FLAVIA. This is a wedding. We're forgetting our
programme. It's time for dancing.

(*MUSIC. Gradually couples form and begin to dance.*

*BOGDAN and IRINA, MIHAI and FLAVIA, FLORINA
and RADU, LUCIA and IANOŞ.*
GABRIEL tries to dance on his crutch.
*For some time they dance in silence. The ANGEL and
VAMPIRE are there, dancing together. They begin to
enjoy themselves.*
*Then they start to talk while they dance, sometimes to
their partner and sometimes to one of the others, at first
a sentence or two and finally all talking at once. The
sentences are numbered in a suggested order. At 14,
every couple talks at once, with each person alternating
lines with their partner and overlapping with their
partner at the end. So that by the end everyone is
talking at once but leaving the vampire's last four or
five words to be heard alone. At first they talk quietly
then more freely, some angry, some exuberant. They
speak Romanian.)*

BOGDAN.
1. Țara asta are nevoie de un bărbat puternic. (This
country needs a strong man.)
5. Sîntem un gunoi (We're garbage.)
13. Dă-le una peste gură. (Smack them in the mouth.)
Ei știu lucruri pe care nimeni altcineva nu le știe,
păsări, broaște, vaci, dumnezeu, direcția vîntului. (They
know things nobody else knows, birds, frogs, cows, god,
the direction of the wind.)

IRINA.
3. Ea spune ca noi nu avem suflet. (She says we have
no soul.)

12. (El) ar trebui spinzurat într-o cuşcă, să dea lumea cu pietre în el. (He should have been hung up in a cage and stones thrown at him.)

14. Tu n-o să te măriţi cu-n ungur. (You're not going to marry a Hungarian.) Datorită lui Gaby poţi să vorbeşti aşa. (It's thanks to Gaby you can talk like this.)

MIHAI.

8. Nimic nu e pe baze realistice. (Nothing is on a realistic basis.)

Trebuie să lăsăm trecutul în spate. (We have to put the past behind us.)

Frontul doreşte sa înlesnească democraţia. (The Front wish to facilitate democracy.)

Ei nu vor aranja votarea, fiindcă ştiu ei că vor învinge. (They wouldn't fix the vote because they knew they were going to win.)

FLAVIA.

2. Nu este istoria ce e în cartea de istorie? (Isn't history what's in the history books?)

14. Vreau să predau corect. (I wish to teach correctly.) Unde sînt casetele? (Where are the tapes?)

Voi scrie o istorie adevarată, ca să ştim exact ce s-a întîmplat. (I'm going to write a true history so we'll know exactly what happened.)

Am votat cu liberalii. (I voted Liberal.)

FLORINA.

4. Uneori îmi este dor de el. (Sometimes I miss him.)

14. Doctorul şef a încuiat răniţii într-o camera. (The head doctor locked the wounded in a room.)

Comuniştii nu trebuie să candideze în alegeri. (The communists shouldn't stand in the election.)

Imi place să fiu obosită, nu-mi place să te aud vorbind.
(I like being tired, I don't like listening to you talk.)

RADU.
9. Cine a tras în douazeci și doi? Nu e o întrebare
absurdă. (Who was shooting on the 22nd? That's not a
crazy question.)

Cine a aruncat pocnitori? Cine a adus difuzoare? (Who
let off firecrackers? Who brought loudhailers?)

Nu-mi pasă cum se numesc, este același popor. (I don't
care what they're called it's the same people.)

Trădezi morţii. (You're betraying the dead.)

LUCIA.
11. Mi-a fost rușine ca nu am fost acolo. (I was so
ashamed not to be here.)

14. Dar ce inseamna asta? De ce parte a fost el? (But
what does it mean? Whose side was he on?) De ce n-au
școlile lor? (Why shouldn't they have their own schools?)

Nu sint sclava ta. (I'm not your slave.)

IANOȘ.
7. Ești acuzat de genocid. (You're on trial for genocide.)

Cine este opozitia? Ungurii. (Who's the opposition?
Hungarians.)

Voi aţi fost prea mult sub turci, sînteţi ca sclavii. (You
were under the Turks too long, you're like slaves.)

Vreau sa invăţ tot. (I want to learn everything.)

GABRIEL.
10. Sînt așa de fericit, ca sînt de cealaltă parte. (I'm so
happy I've put myself on the other side.)

14. Diferit acum. (Different now.)

Ii urasc pe francezi. (I hate the French.)

Ungurii îi fac pe oameni să ne disprețuiască. (The Hungarians make people despise us.)

Aș vrea să fi fost omorît. Glumesc. (I wish I'd been killed. Just joking.)

ANGEL.

6. Să nu-ți fie rușine. (Don't be ashamed.)

13. Nu libertatea din afară ci libertatea interioară. (Not outer freedom of course but inner freedom.)

Am încercat sa mă țin departe de politică. (I try to keep clear of the political side.)

Zburînd in albastru. (Flying about in the blue.)

VAMPIRE.

11. Nu-ți fie frică. (Don't be frightened.)

14. Nu sînt o ființă umană. (I'm not a human being.)

Incepi să vrei sînge. Membrele te dor, capul îți arde. Trebuie să te miști din ce în ce mai repede. (You begin to want blood. Your limbs ache, your head burns, you have to keep moving faster and faster.)

.

Technical Layout of III/8

3.

IRINA. She and her followers talk without speaking, they know each other's thoughts. She just looks at you and she knows your troubles. I told her all about Gaby. [1]

LUCIA. So you told her your troubles. No wonder she knows.

IRINA. When they send him to Italy for his operation maybe we won't need a psychic. She said I could take him to see her. [2]

LUCIA. He'll just laugh.

IRINA. She says we have no soul. We've suffered for so many years and we don't know how to live. Are people very different in other countries, Lucia?

LUCIA. Cheer up, have a drink. It's Florina's wedding day. [7]

IRINA. I'll miss Florina.

4.

LUCIA *is talking to a smiling* WAITER. [5]

WAITER. I remember your wedding last year. That was a very different time. We had bugs in the vases. Still. Can I help you change some dollars?

LUCIA. No thank you.

WAITER. I used to help your husband. It's easier now. My brother's gone to Switzerland to buy a Mercedes. You're sure I can't help you? Top rate, high as Everest.

LUCIA. Thank you but I don't have any dollars left. [6]

The WAITER*'s smile disappears.*

1.

FLAVIA. What's so wonderful about a wedding is everyone laughs and cries and it's like the revolution again. Because everyone's gone back behind their masks. Don't you think so?

BOGDAN. I don't know. Perhaps. You could say that.

2.

MIHAI. I forgot to take my windshield wipers off last night so of course they've been stolen. Still, my son doesn't get married every day.

7.

FLORINA. I thought I was going to get the giggles.

RADU. It was good though.

FLORINA. It was lovely.

5.

BOGDAN. I know someone at work killed his son-in-law. He put an axe in his head. Then he put a knife in the dead man's hand to make like it was self-defence, and said anyway he wasn't there, it was his son. And he got away with it. Smart, huh? [a]

RADU. What happened to the son? [b] [c]

BOGDAN. Luckily he had some money, he only got six years.

RADU. What's he going to do to his dad when he gets out?

They laugh.

6.

FLAVIA. [a] How's your little brother?

IANOŞ. [b] He wakes up in the night now and cries.

FLAVIA. [c] How's your mother?

They laugh.

8.

IANOŞ. Lucia and I are going to start a newspaper.

LUCIA. A friend's sending us magazines from America and we'll translate interesting articles. 9

IANOŞ (*to* LUCIA). Do people really dress like in Vogue?

10.

IANOŞ. A French doctor told me 4000 babies / have it.

GABRIEL. I hate the French, they're so superior.

IANOŞ. Yes, they do like to help.

GABRIEL. Merci, merci.

IANOŞ. Can you really sterilise infected needles with alcohol? 10A

GABRIEL. I'm sterilising myself with alcohol.

9.

IRINA. I bought these shoes in the street.

FLAVIA. Did they want dollars?

IRINA. Yes, Lucia's last dollars were spent on the wedding.

FLAVIA. Black market prices have shot up.

IRINA. It's not black market, it's free market.

11. *Old peasant* AUNT *shouts ritual chants at* FLORINA.

AUNT. Little bride, little bride,
You're laughing, we've cried.
Now a man's come to choose you
We're sad because we lose you— 10
Makes you proud to be a wife
But it's not an easy life.
Your husband isn't like a brother
Your mother-in-law's not like a mother.
More fun running free and wild
Than staying home to mind a child.
Better to be on the shelf
Only have to please yourself— 10A
Little bride don't be sad,
Not to marry would be mad.
Single girls are all in tears,
They'll be lonely many years.
Lovely girl you're like a flower, /
Only pretty for an hour -

BOGDAN. Stop it, auntie, you're not on the farm now.

FLORINA. No, I like it. Go on.

1.

IRINA. If only he'd stayed in University Square.

LUCIA. He could have been shot there. ③

IRINA. The bullets missed Ianoş.

LUCIA. Do you wish they'd hit him?

IRINA. No but of course anyone else.

2.

FLORINA. Be nice to your mom and dad.

RADU. I am nice.

4.

FLAVIA. I'm going to write a true history, Florina, so we'll know exactly what happened. How much do you think Moscow was involved / in planning the coup?

FLORINA. I don't know. I don't care. I'm sorry.

FLAVIA. What did you vote? Liberal?

FLORINA. Yes of course. ⑦

FLAVIA. So did I, so did I.

She hugs FLORINA. ⑤

Mihai doesn't know. And next time we'll win. Jos Iliescu.

6.

JANOS. Have another drink.

LUCIA. I've had another drink.

JANOS. Have another other drink.

They laugh.

3

BOGDAN. Bitch, bitch. Gaby was shot, all right. Everyone bitches. Layabout students. Radu and Ianos never stop talking, ② want to smack them in the mouth. 'Was it a revolution?' Of course it was. / My son was shot for it and we've got

MIHAI. Certainly. Of course .

BOGDAN. This country needs a strong man. ④

MIHAI. And we've got one.

BOGDAN. We've got one. Iliescu's a strong man. We can't have a traffic jam forever. Are they going to clear the square or not?

MIHAI. The government has to avoid any action that would give credibility to the current unsubstantiated allegations.

BOGDAN. They're weak, aren't they.

7.

IRINA. Ceauşescu shouldn't have been shot. ⑨

RADU. Because he would have exposed people / in the Front.

IRINA. He should have been hung up in a cage and stones thrown at him.

They laugh. ⑥

5.

RADU. Look at Gaby, crippled for nothing. They've voted the same bunch in.

IRINA. It's thanks to Gaby you can talk like this. ⑩ ⟶

8.

BOGDAN. (to MIHAI). If Radu had been hurt instead of Gaby, he'd be in that hospital in Italy by now.

10.

IRINA. I don't like seeing you with Ianoş.

LUCIA. He's Gabriel's friend. [12]

IRINA. I was once in a shop in Transylvania and they wouldn't serve me because I couldn't speak Hungarian. / In my own county.

LUCIA. Yes, but –

IRINA. And what if the doctor only spoke Hungarian / and someone wanted a doctor?

BOGDAN. Stuck-up bastards.

IRINA. Are you going back to America? You're not going back.

LUCIA. Didn't you miss me?

IRINA. Aren't you ashamed? Two years of hell to get your precious American and you don't even want him. Did he beat you?

LUCIA. I got homesick.

IRINA. Was Ianoş going on before?

LUCIA. Of course not. You didn't think that?

IRINA. I don't know what I thought. I just made the wedding dress. [1]

LUCIA. You like Ianoş.

IRINA. Go back to America, Lucia, and maybe we can all go. You owe us that.

BOGDAN. You're a slut, Lucia.

9.

GABRIEL. I can't work. Rodica can't work. What's going to happen to us? I wish I'd been killed.

FLORINA. You're going to Italy.

GABRIEL. When? Can't you do something to hurry things up, Florina? Sleep with a doctor? Just joking.

13.

FLORINA. I'm glad about you and Ianoş.

They kiss.

Tell me something.

LUCIA. Don't ask.

FLORINA. No, tell me.

LUCIA. Two years is a long time when you hardly know somebody. I'd lost my job, I had to go through with it, I wanted to get away. [Ba] [Rb]

FLORINA. But you loved Wayne at first? If you didn't I'll kill you.

LUCIA. Of course I did. But don't tell Ianoş.

12.

MIHAI. I was in the British Embassy library reading the Architect's Journal and there's a building in Japan forty stories high with a central atrium up to twenty stories. So the problem is how to get light into the central volume. The German engineer has an ingenious solution where they've installed computerised mirrors angled to follow the sun so they reflect natural light into the atrium according to the season and the time of day, so you have sunlight in a completely enclosed space. [1]

11.

FLAVIA. Where are the tapes they made when they listened to everyone talking? All that history wasted. I'd like to find someone in the Securitate who could tell me. Bogdan, do you know anyone?

BOGDAN. Why me?

FLAVIA. I used to know someone but she's disappeared.

BOGDAN. They should be driven into the open and punished. Big public trials. The Front aren't doing their job.

FLAVIA. There wouldn't be enough prisons.

BOGDAN. (to MIHAI). There's a use for your People's Palace.

14.

PRIEST. You can't blame anybody. Everyone was trying to survive. [B]

BOGDAN. Wipe them out. Even if it's the entire population. We're garbage. The Front are stuck-up bastards. They'd have to wipe themselves out too.

PRIEST. We have to try to love our enemies.

BOGDAN. Plenty of enemies. So we must be the most loving people in the world. Did you love him? Give him a kiss would you? [Ba]

PRIEST. When I say love. It's enough not to hate.

BOGDAN. Handy for you having God say be nice to Ceauşescu. [Bb]

PRIEST. You're your own worst enemy, Bogdan.

BOGDAN. So I ought to love myself best.

PRIEST. Don't hate yourself anyway.

BOGDAN. Why not? Don't you? You're a smug fuck.

2. MIHAI, RADU and FLORINA, joined by FLAVIA.

MIHAI.   The Front wouldn't fix the vote because they knew they were going to win. Everyone appreciates the sacrifice made by youth. The revolution is in safe hands. This isn't a day for worrying, Florina and Radu, you take too much on. I wish you could let it all go for a little while. Please believe me, I want your happiness.

| 1a |
| 3 |

FLORINA.   We know you do.

She kisses him.

RADU.   Yes, I know. I appreciate that.

MIHAI.   After all, I'm not a monster. Most of the country supports the Front. It's only in my own home it takes courage to say it. We have a government of reconciliation.

FLAVIA.   Why don't the Front tell the truth and admit they're communists? / * Nothing to be

MIHAI.   Because they're not.

RADU.   * I don't care what they're called, it's the same people.

FLAVIA.   ashamed of in communism, / nothing to be

FLORINA.   They should have been banned / from

MIHAI.   That's your idea of freedom, banning people?

FLORINA.   running in the election.

RADU.   We've got to have another revolution.

FLAVIA.   ashamed of in planning the revolution if they'd just admit it. You never dared speak out against Ceauşescu, Mihai, and you don't dare speak out now. Say it, I'm a communist and so what. / Say it, I'm a communist.

RADU.   Jos comunismul, jos comunismul. / Jos Iliescu. Jos tiranul. Jos Iliescu. Jos Iliescu.

FLORINA.   Radu, don't be childish.

BOGDAN joins in shouting 'Jos comunismul', then turns his attention to the other group.

1.

BOGDAN.   a. Private schools, private hospitals. I've seen what happens to old people. I want to buy my father a decent death.

| 2. |

b. I support the Peasants Party because my father's a peasant. I'm not ashamed of that. They should have their land because their feet are in the earth and they know things nobody else knows. Birds, frogs, cows, god, the direction of the wind.

| b. |

c. CIA, KGB, we're all in the hands of foreign agents. That's one point where I'm right behind Ceauşescu.

| 0. |

3. GABRIEL at first in group with MIHAI, IANOŞ and IRINA then with LUCIA, IANOŞ and IRINA.

GABRIEL.   The only reason we need an internal security force is if Hungary tried to invade us / we'd need to be sure -

LUCIA.   Invade? are you serious?

IANOŞ.   When we get Transylvania back it's going to be legally / because it's ours.

IRINA.   You're not going to marry a Hungarian.

LUCIA.   I'm married already. | 1b |

IANOŞ.   Gaby, the Hungarians started the revolution. Without us you'd still be worshipping Ceauşescu. / And now the

GABRIEL jeers

LUCIA.   We didn't worship him.

IRINA.   Gaby's a hero, Ianoş.

IANOŞ.   Romanians worship Iliescu. Who's the opposition? Hungarians.

GABRIEL.   That's just voting for your language.

LUCIA.   Why shouldn't they have their own schools?

IRINA.   And lock Romanian children out in the street. If it wasn't bad enough you going to America, now a Hungarian, / and Gaby crippled, and Radu's irresponsible, I worry for Florina.

GABRIEL.   If they want to live in Romania / they can

LUCIA.   In the riots on TV I saw a Hungarian on the

GABRIEL.   speak Romanian.

IANOŞ.   We can learn two languages, we're not stupid.

LUCIA.   ground and Romanians kicking him.

GABRIEL.   That was a Romanian on the ground, and Hungarians – you think we're stupid?

IANOŞ.   You were under the Turks too long, it made you like slaves.

LUCIA.   You think I'm a slave? I'm not your slave.

GABRIEL pushes IANOŞ, who pushes him back. BOGDAN arrives.

BOGDAN.   Leave my son alone. Hungarian bastard. And don't come near my daughter.

IANOŞ.   I'm already fucking your daughter, you stupid peasant.

BOGDAN hits IANOŞ.
RADU restrains BOGDAN.
LUCIA attacks BOGDAN.
BOGDAN hits RADU.
MIHAI pushes BOGDAN.
BOGDAN hits MIHAI.
FLAVIA attacks BOGDAN.
IANOŞ pushes GABRIEL.
IRINA protects GABRIEL.
GABRIEL hits IANOŞ.
RADU attacks BOGDAN.
MIHAI restrains RADU.
RADU attacks MIHAI.
FLORINA attacks RADU.
GABRIEL hits out indiscriminately with his crutch and accidentally knocks BOGDAN to the floor.

Stunned silence.

FLAVIA.   This is a wedding. We're forgetting our programme. It's time for dancing.

Also By
Caryl Churchill

Abortive

Cloud 9

Fen

Ice Cream with Hot Fudge

Light Shining in Buckinghamshire

Lovesick

Mad Forest

Not Not Not Not Not Enough Oxygen

Owners

Schreber's Nervous Illness

Seagulls

Three More Sleepless Nights

Traps

Vinegar Tom

Please visit our website **samuelfrench.com** for complete descriptions and licensing information

ABORTIVE

Caryl Churchill

Drama / 1m, 1f / Interior

Roz and Colin are having a difficult time with sex, largely because of an invisible yet forbidding barrier between them. Roz became pregnant after being raped and had an abortion. Roz is not sure she made the right decision and Colin is not altogether convinced his wife was raped. In *Churchill: Shorts.*

OTHER TITLES AVAILABLE FROM SAMUEL FRENCH

THE RIVERS AND RAVINES
Heather McDonald

Drama / 9m, 5f / Unit Set

Originally produced to acclaim by Washington D.C.'s famed Arena Stage. This is an engrossing political drama about the contemporary farm crisis in America and its effect on rural communities.

"A haunting and emotionally draining play. A community of farmers and ranchers in a small Colorado town disintegrates under the weight of failure and thwarted ambitions. Most of the farmers, their spouses, children, clergyman, banker and greasy spoon proprietress survive, but it is survival without triumph. This is an *Our Town* for the 80's."
— *The Washington Post*